PREVENTING
TEEN MOTOR CRASHES

CONTRIBUTIONS FROM THE BEHAVIORAL AND SOCIAL SCIENCES

W O R K S H O P   R E P O R T

Program Committee for a Workshop on Contributions from the
Behavioral and Social Sciences in
Reducing and Preventing Teen Motor Crashes

Board on Children, Youth, and Families
Division of Behavioral and Social Sciences and Education
Institute of Medicine

and the

Transportation Research Board

NATIONAL RESEARCH COUNCIL,
INSTITUTE OF MEDICINE, *AND*
TRANSPORTATION RESEARCH BOARD
OF THE NATIONAL ACADEMIES

THE NATIONAL ACADEMIES PRESS
Washington, D.C.
www.nap.edu

THE NATIONAL ACADEMIES PRESS 500 Fifth Street, N.W. Washington, DC 20001

NOTICE: The project that is the subject of this report was approved by the Governing Board of the National Research Council, whose members are drawn from the councils of the National Academy of Sciences, the National Academy of Engineering, and the Institute of Medicine. The members of the committee responsible for the report were chosen for their special competences and with regard for appropriate balance.

This study was supported by Award Nos. N01-OD-4-2139, 200-2000-00629, and UPVT-7578 between the National Academy of Sciences and the National Institutes of Health, the Centers for Disease Control and Prevention, and the State Farm Insurance Companies®. Any opinions, findings, conclusions, or recommendations expressed in this publication are those of the author(s) and do not necessarily reflect the views of the organizations or agencies that provided support for the project.

International Standard Book Number 13: 978-0-309-10401-2
International Standard Book Number 10: 0-309-10401-7

Additional copies of this report are available from The National Academies Press, 500 Fifth Street, N.W., Lockbox 285, Washington, DC 20055; (800) 624-6242 or (202) 334-3313 (in the Washington metropolitan area); Internet, http://www.nap.edu

Printed in the United States of America

Suggested citation: National Research Council, Institute of Medicine, and Transportation Research Board. (2007). *Preventing Teen Motor Crashes: Contributions from the Behavioral and Social Sciences, Workshop Report.* Program Committee for a Workshop on Contributions from the Behavioral and Social Sciences in Reducing and Preventing Teen Motor Crashes. Washington, DC: The National Academies Press.

THE NATIONAL ACADEMIES
Advisers to the Nation on Science, Engineering, and Medicine

The **National Academy of Sciences** is a private, nonprofit, self-perpetuating society of distinguished scholars engaged in scientific and engineering research, dedicated to the furtherance of science and technology and to their use for the general welfare. Upon the authority of the charter granted to it by the Congress in 1863, the Academy has a mandate that requires it to advise the federal government on scientific and technical matters. Dr. Ralph J. Cicerone is president of the National Academy of Sciences.

The **National Academy of Engineering** was established in 1964, under the charter of the National Academy of Sciences, as a parallel organization of outstanding engineers. It is autonomous in its administration and in the selection of its members, sharing with the National Academy of Sciences the responsibility for advising the federal government. The National Academy of Engineering also sponsors engineering programs aimed at meeting national needs, encourages education and research, and recognizes the superior achievements of engineers. Dr. Wm. A. Wulf is president of the National Academy of Engineering.

The **Institute of Medicine** was established in 1970 by the National Academy of Sciences to secure the services of eminent members of appropriate professions in the examination of policy matters pertaining to the health of the public. The Institute acts under the responsibility given to the National Academy of Sciences by its congressional charter to be an adviser to the federal government and, upon its own initiative, to identify issues of medical care, research, and education. Dr. Harvey V. Fineberg is president of the Institute of Medicine.

The **National Research Council** was organized by the National Academy of Sciences in 1916 to associate the broad community of science and technology with the Academy's purposes of furthering knowledge and advising the federal government. Functioning in accordance with general policies determined by the Academy, the Council has become the principal operating agency of both the National Academy of Sciences and the National Academy of Engineering in providing services to the government, the public, and the scientific and engineering communities. The Council is administered jointly by both Academies and the Institute of Medicine. Dr. Ralph J. Cicerone and Dr. Wm. A. Wulf are chair and vice chair, respectively, of the National Research Council.

www.national-academies.org

PROGRAM COMMITTEE FOR A WORKSHOP ON CONTRIBUTIONS FROM THE BEHAVIORAL AND SOCIAL SCIENCES IN REDUCING AND PREVENTING TEEN MOTOR CRASHES

ROBERT GRAHAM (*Chair*), Department of Family Medicine, College of Medicine, University of Cincinnati

BRIAN K. BARBER, Department of Child and Family Studies, University of Tennessee, Knoxville

CLAIRE D. BRINDIS, National Adolescent Health Information Center, University of California, San Francisco

B. BRADFORD BROWN, Department of Educational Psychology, University of Wisconsin–Madison

WILLIAM DEJONG, School of Public Health, Boston University

DONALD L. FISHER, Human Performance Laboratory, University of Massachusetts, Amherst

BONNIE L. HALPERN-FELSHER, Department of Pediatrics, University of California, San Francisco

DANIEL P. KEATING, Center for Human Growth and Development, University of Michigan, Ann Arbor

JOHN D. LEE, Department of Mechanical and Industrial Engineering, University of Iowa, Iowa City

DANIEL R. MAYHEW, Traffic Injury Research Foundation, Ottawa, Ontario

CAROL W. RUNYAN, Injury Prevention Research Center, University of North Carolina, Chapel Hill

JEAN THATCHER SHOPE, Transportation Research Institute, University of Michigan, Ann Arbor

ALLAN F. WILLIAMS, consultant, Bethesda, Maryland

FLAURA KOPLIN WINSTON, Center for Injury Research and Prevention, Children's Hospital of Philadelphia

ALEXANDRA BEATTY, *Rapporteur*
JENNIFER APPLETON GOOTMAN, *Study Director*
APRIL HIGGINS, *Senior Program Assistant*
WENDY KEENAN, *Program Associate*
RICK PAIN, Transportation Safety Coordinator

Contents

Preface

The Board on Children, Youth, and Families (BCYF) of the National Research Council (NRC) and the Institute of Medicine has organized a series of planning meetings, workshops, and consensus studies over the past decade that address different facets of adolescent health and development (see the BCYF web site: www.bocyf.org). In the midst of this work, the board identified a significant omission: the work of researchers with new insights and understanding of teen risk behaviors and adolescent development in general had not yet been systematically applied to key policy, education, or practice questions related to the problem of teen crashes.

Following a series of tragic deaths involving teen drivers and passengers in metropolitan Washington, DC, in October 2004, the Committee on Adolescent Health and Development reviewed the emerging research on teen driving. It concluded that the time was ripe to examine this work within a broad interdisciplinary forum involving experts from fields of study that had remained apart for too long. BCYF pursued this initiative in collaboration with the Transportation Research Board of the National Academies, which has a long and robust history of addressing highway safety through convening interdisciplinary conferences and workshops, identifying and sponsoring research, and influencing policy through studies in highway safety conducted at the request of Congress and the executive branch.

From this internal consultation emerged a proposal for a national workshop that would bring together traffic safety experts with others from a broad array of disciplines, including researchers who study adolescent health, injury prevention, public health, youth development, risk assessment, behavioral psychology, and other fields of social and behavioral study that examine interactions that influence today's youth. The workshop was viewed as just a beginning—an opportunity for a diverse group to examine how research findings from a broad array of disciplines could be presented within an interdisciplinary framework and integrated in ways that could address a critical public health need, improve the quality of prevention strategies, and ultimately reduce teen motor vehicle crashes and save lives. This report, which summarizes what took place at the workshop, can serve only to introduce readers to the potential connections among work on adolescent development from the behavioral and social sciences and research findings from the fields of traffic safety and public health. It is not intended as a comprehensive summary of the existing body of literature on either teen driving or adolescent development, nor does it make any specific recommendations. Instead, like the workshop itself, it is intended as a spur to further action.

We greatly appreciate the public- and private-sector partnership that emerged to support this undertaking. The Office of Behavioral and Social Science Research in the National Institutes of Health, the National Center for Injury Prevention and Control at the Centers for Disease Control and Prevention (CDC), and the State Farm Insurance Companies® sponsored the workshop project and provided technical assistance in key areas of interest. Particular acknowledgment is given to Bruce Simons-Morton from the National Institute for Child Health and Human Development, Ruth Shults from CDC, and John Nepomuceno from State Farm Insurance Companies®, each of whom offered guidance and encouragement during the formative stages of this activity.

The two-day workshop summarized in this report was held at the National Academies in May 2006. The workshop made possible expert presentation of new research findings from the social, behavioral, and health sciences, as well as opportunities to engage in broad interdisciplinary dialogue about the implications of this research. Apart from the expertise of the speakers and members of the program committee, the participants included others with a wide array of expertise in traffic safety and adolescent health interests, as well as stakeholders concerned with improving the quality of life for today's youth—including parents whose lives have been touched by the tragedy of motor vehicle crash fatalities.

It was difficult indeed to condense the rich array of research literature into a two-day program. We are particularly grateful for the contributions of the expert presenters who helped to structure the workshop program, as well as the other discussants and participants who contributed to the discussions (see Appendix A for the workshop agenda and list of presenters). Many of the speakers and participants were eager to see additional activity emerge from this initial discussion; all welcomed the opportunity to meet with new colleagues and to reframe their work in a setting that encouraged moving beyond the traditional confines of disciplinary inquiry.

Members of the program committee met once to plan and convene the workshop, and they met again immediately after the gathering to identify major themes to be presented in this summary report. In preparing the report, the workshop rapporteur, Alexandra Beatty, assisted in synthesizing the key points. Special appreciation also goes to members of the project staff, including Jennifer Appleton Gootman, study director; Rick Pain, transportation safety coordinator; and Wendy Keenan, program associate, who ably assisted with the organization of the meeting.

This report summarizes the committee's assessment of what transpired at the workshop and highlights some of the views expressed by workshop speakers or participants. While the committee is responsible for the overall quality and accuracy of the report as a record of what transpired at the workshop, the views of workshop participants whose comments are summarized are not necessarily those of the planning committee members.

This workshop report has been reviewed in draft form by individuals chosen for their diverse perspectives and technical expertise, in accordance with procedures approved by the Report Review Committee of the National Research Council. The purpose of this independent review is to provide candid and critical comments that will assist the institution in making its published report as sound as possible and to ensure that the report meets institutional standards for objectivity, evidence, and responsiveness to the charge. The review comments and draft manuscript remain confidential to protect the integrity of the process. We thank the following individuals for their review of this report: Susan S. Gallagher, Children's Safety Network, Education Development Center, Newton, MA; Jay N. Giedd, Child and Adolescent Psychiatrist, Potomac, MD; Ricardo Martinez, Medical Affairs, The Schumacher Group, Kennesaw, GA; John W. Palmer, Health and Safety, St. Cloud State University; Dan Romer, Annenberg Public Policy Center, University of Pennsylvania; Teresa M. Senserrick, Center for Injury Research and Prevention, The Children's Hospital of Philadelphia; and Jerry Wachtel, Office of the President, The Veridian Group, Inc., Berkeley, CA.

Although the reviewers listed above provided many constructive comments and suggestions, they were not asked to endorse the content of the report, nor did they see the final draft of the report before its release. The review of this report was overseen by Laurence Steinberg, Department of Psychology, Temple University. Appointed by the National Research Council, he was responsible for making certain that an independent examination of this report was carried out in accordance with institutional procedures and that all review comments were carefully considered. Responsibility for the final content of this report rests entirely with the authoring committee and the institution.

Rosemary Chalk, *Director*
Board on Children, Youth, and Families

1

Introduction:
A Critical Public Health Problem

In July 2003, Joshua Brown, a high school senior from Cartersville, Georgia, who had recently been accepted by the Berklee School of Music, was killed in a car crash. His death was tragic for his family, and it represents a tragic loss for the nation. Joshua was one of 3,657 young drivers who died in car crashes in the United States in 2003. When the additional deaths of teen passengers and pedestrians are included, motor vehicle crashes emerge as the leading cause of death for this age group in that year (accounting for 5,988 deaths among youth ages 16 to 20). These crashes were responsible for more adolescent deaths than the next four causes combined (National Center for Health Statistics, 2003).[1]

Young people in the United States are at greater risk of dying or being injured in an automobile than their peers around the world, in part because they are licensed to drive earlier and with less experience than youth in other countries (Insurance Institute for Highway Safety, 2006).[2] If current

---

[1] The next four leading causes of death in 2003 for youth ages 16 to 20 were homicide (2,489), suicide (1,813), accidental poisoning (752), and malignant neoplasms (749) (National Center for Health Statistics, 2003).

[2] The risks of teen driving are nevertheless a serious concern in other countries, and a significant body of research from other countries exists. While there was not time to explore the contributions from this research at the workshop, interested readers are directed to a September 2006 report titled *Young Drivers: The Road to Safety*, prepared by the Transport Research Centre, a collaborative venture of the Organisation for Economic Co-operation and Development and the European Conference of Ministers of Transport.

trends continue, a cumulative total of more than 100,000 adolescents and young adults (ages 16 to 24) who are alive today will die in car crashes in the next 10 years (Winston and Senserrick, 2006).[3] Furthermore, nearly two of every three people killed in teen-driver crashes are people other than the teen driver (American Automobile Association, 2006). By any measure, then, automobile crashes are one of the most critical public health problems in the United States.

After Joshua's death, his parents dedicated themselves to combating this problem, and they were by no means the first. States, counties, and school districts; the federal government; private organizations, such as the Insurance Institute for Highway Safety; advocacy groups, such as Mothers Against Drunk Driving; and others have addressed the problem in a variety of ways. Fatalities and injuries overall and for teenagers have been reduced substantially over the past 30 years as a result of changes in state laws, such as seat belt requirements and increases in the legal drinking age (National Highway Traffic Safety Administration, 2006a). Changes in licensure requirements, public information campaigns, and strategies for encouraging parent involvement in the training of new drivers are other valuable strategies that have been used to improve driving safety for teens. While the impact of these efforts is evident, novice drivers continue to have the highest rates of crashes, injuries, and fatalities of any group; the sheer magnitude of the injuries and fatalities that continue to result from teen crashes shows that current prevention efforts are inadequate.

Knowledge about how and why teen motor vehicle crashes happen is the key to developing countermeasures to reduce their number—and a significant body of applicable knowledge, produced over several decades, exists. However, few effective mechanisms are available for using that knowledge to directly influence teen behavior or to convert it into effective interventions. In addition, many of the efforts to reduce teen crashes that are in place are hampered by a lack of evidence as to which prevention strategies are most effective. Driving is a complex activity, mastery of which develops slowly over time, despite the fact that for most adults it seems largely automatic. It is a social activity as well as one that draws on a com-

---

[3]Estimate based on an analysis of 2003 data for adolescents and young adults (ages 16 to 24) from the Fatality Analysis Reporting System (FARS). Fatality information derived from FARS includes motor vehicle traffic crashes that result in the death of an occupant of a vehicle or a nonmotorist within 30 days of the crash.

plex array of physical and cognitive abilities that are still developing in teenagers. Moreover, driving is a skill that adolescents need to learn—the aim of public health efforts is not to prevent the activity altogether (as it is with many other public health initiatives) but to help teens do it more responsibly.

Consequently, an understanding of teenage driving would be enhanced by a systematic review of contributions from the behavioral, cognitive, social, health, and biological sciences. These disciplines have shed light on distinctive aspects of teenagers: their approach to risk assessment, learning processes, skill development, brain functioning, reward incentives, and interactions with peers and adults. Applying this understanding to the development of prevention strategies holds significant promise for improving safety.

While many fields of research have already produced studies that are relevant to this topic, this body of knowledge has not been synthesized in ways that allow key findings to be applied effectively in policy and practice. Furthermore, opportunities for collaboration among researchers from diverse fields to address questions about teenage driving are rare. Research studies are often published in specialized journals that are not widely read by others working in different disciplines or diverse professional environments, and current citation indexing systems make it difficult to integrate research from fields as diverse as public health, traffic safety, adolescent development, and social psychology.

To address this void, the Board on Children, Youth, and Families, under the auspices of the National Research Council and the Institute of Medicine, and in collaboration with the Transportation Research Board, formed the Committee on Contributions from the Behavioral and Social Sciences in Reducing and Preventing Teen Motor Crashes to plan a workshop at which experts from the relevant fields could share information and consider ways to put their combined expertise to work. The committee met in person and collaborated extensively by phone and electronic mail to review the kinds of evidence that are available and identify objectives for the workshop as well as the experts who could best help meet them. The committee was not charged with developing specific recommendations regarding ways to reduce teen motor crashes, but rather with exploring three questions:

1. How do theories and evidence from the behavioral, cognitive, social, health, and biological sciences inform understanding of both the risk

factors that increase teen motor vehicle crashes and the protective factors that reduce such crashes?

2. How can theories and evidence from the behavioral, cognitive, social, health, and biological sciences inform improved prevention, program, and policy interventions to reduce risky teen motor vehicle driving behaviors, as well as promote responsible teen driving?

3. What research and interventions are most likely to advance teen motor vehicle safety over the short and the long term?

The workshop planned to address these questions, held May 15 and 16, 2006, assembled a multidisciplinary group who shared information and insights on topics ranging from adolescent development to emerging technology for studying, monitoring, and controlling driving behavior. The workshop program was structured to bring together researchers who had not addressed studies of teen driving, but who might have unique insights in the field of adolescent development and other areas of social and behavioral research, with experts who have deep experience in the field of highway safety. Presenters laid out aspects of the problem and addressed some of the challenges that face policy makers, and participants engaged in extensive discussion of the implications of the data presented and possible ways forward. A workshop agenda and a complete list of participants appear in the appendix to this report.

This report documents the information presented at the workshop and the discussions that took place. Its purpose is to lay out the key ideas that emerged from the workshop, both for researchers interested in interdisciplinary work in this area and for those who are involved in developing prevention strategies. The report should be viewed as only a first step in exploring opportunities to develop a synthesis of diverse research and applying this knowledge to the problem of preventing teen crashes, and it is confined to the material presented by the workshop speakers. Neither the workshop nor this report is intended as a comprehensive review of what is known about teen driving. Many important topics—such as the potential of insurance incentives or law enforcement practices to strengthen prevention strategies—were not addressed in the limited time available for the workshop. A more comprehensive review and synthesis of relevant research knowledge, including lessons learned from the experiences of other countries, will have to wait for further development.

The report is organized to provide both an overview of the factual information that was presented as well as insights that emerged about the role that researchers can play in reducing and preventing teen motor vehicle crashes. Chapter 2 provides an exploration of teen crashes, how they happen, and the risk factors that contribute to them. Chapter 3 addresses specific features of adolescence that may play a role in the way teenagers drive and their high crash risk. Chapter 4 explores the strategies already being used to improve teenagers' safety on the road, as well as promising strategies not yet being fully implemented. The report closes with a discussion of future directions—Chapter 5 addresses both the need for ongoing research to address pressing questions that have not yet been resolved or have emerged from technological developments, as well as the vital importance of coordinating and capitalizing on an already impressive body of knowledge about teen driving.

2

The Anatomy of Crashes Involving Young Drivers

An understanding of how the number of teen crashes might be reduced begins with an understanding of how they happen. Many of the speakers presented data that shed light not only on the strikingly large scope of the problem, but also on what goes wrong when teenagers have crashes.

THE GRAVEST PUBLIC HEALTH PROBLEM FOR YOUNG DRIVERS

Driving is dangerous, and especially so for new drivers. Motor vehicle crashes are the leading cause of mortality and serious morbidity for all young people ages 4 through 34, and the rates are highest during new drivers' first few months of driving on their own. In fact, during their first six months of solo driving, newly licensed drivers are about eight times more likely to be involved in fatal crashes than are more experienced drivers (Insurance Institute for Highway Safety, 2004). Even after more than six months licensed to drive alone, teens are two to three times more likely to be in a fatal crash than are the most experienced drivers. The overall numbers are alarming—by one analysis, more than 100,000 young people (ages 16 to 24) will die in vehicle crashes between 2003 and 2012 if the crash rates do not change, as shown in Table 2-1.

Crash rates are significantly higher for male than female drivers, but while overall rates are increasing, young women are catching up with young

TABLE 2-1 Cumulative Total Deaths from Motor
Vehicle Crashes Involving Teen Drivers, 2003 to 2012

Age Group	Projected Cumulative Number of Deaths
16 to 17	20, 896
18 to 19	27, 689
20 to 24	54, 830
Total	103, 415

NOTE: Analysis based on calculations from the Fatality Analysis
Reporting System, 2003 data.
SOURCE: Winston (2006).

men. Moreover, the proportionate mortality rates—that is, the number of
vehicle crash deaths divided by the number of all deaths among 16- to 19-
year-olds—are 36.5 percent for young men and 46.5 percent for young
women (D'Angelo, 2006). The high mortality rates for young drivers (ages
15 to 20) have persisted over the past decade, with an increase of 5 percent
between 1994 and 2004. During this same time period, driver fatalities
rose by 1 percent among young male drivers, compared with a 15 percent
increase for young women, according to data presented by Richard
Compton (National Highway Traffic Safety Administration, 2006a).

Injuries are another significant component of the problem—303,000
young people ages 15 to 20 were injured in crashes in 2004, many of them
very seriously (National Highway Traffic Safety Administration, 2006a).
Moreover, these numbers do not include deaths or injuries of thousands of
other nonteenage drivers, passengers, or pedestrians that occur as a result of
crashes caused by teenage drivers (American Automobile Association,
2006).

From a public health perspective, motor vehicle crashes are among the
most serious problems facing teenagers. Studies by the AAA Foundation
for Traffic Safety indicate that teen drivers are overrepresented in road
crashes, with a higher per-mile collision rate than older drivers (American
Automobile Association, 2006). From an economic perspective, these
crashes also impose an enormous cost to society. It is estimated by the
Centers for Disease Control and Prevention that the 2002 cost of crashes
involving drivers ages 15 to 20 was $40.8 billion (National Center for In-
jury Prevention and Control, 2006). This information can provide a useful

context for discussions of the costs of measures designed to reduce the number of teen crashes.

RISK FACTORS

Just what is it about teenagers that makes them prone to motor vehicle crashes? Jim Hedlund provided a framework for the wealth of data on risk factors for teens by describing five critical elements teens need to drive safely:

- skills—which include the capacity to operate the vehicle and to recognize hazards, as well as the capacity to react appropriately to the unexpected;
- knowledge—of traffic rules and operating procedures, as well as understanding of risks and their potential consequences;
- experience—including both sufficient practice, as well as the familiarity with the consequences of bad judgment that fosters good judgment;
- maturity—or developed capacity for reasoning, judgment, and decision making; and
- environment—or safe surroundings in which to learn to drive.

Whether or not these elements are all in place, teens are eager to drive, and their crash risk is particularly high in the first few months they are on the road, as well as when they travel at night, when teenage passengers are in the car, when they are driving too fast for conditions, and when they have consumed alcohol. Parents often believe that if they could be sure their teenagers would never drink and drive, or ride with someone else who had been drinking, their children would be safe on the road, but, as David Preusser noted, the biggest risk factor for teens is possession of a driver's license. The key reasons why are discussed below.

Youth

Young drivers are at significantly higher risk than older drivers, as we have seen, and there is a learning curve for *all* new drivers, regardless of the age at which they begin driving.[1] Table 2-2 shows the steep decline in crash

---

[1]So-called recalcitrant high-risk drivers, those who are characterized by disregard for authority and a propensity for risk-taking beyond the teen years, have also been identified as

TABLE 2-2 Crash Rates for Novice Drivers per Cumulative Miles Driven After Licensure

Miles Driven After Licensure	Crash Involvement Rate (per 10K cumulative miles)
250	3.2 average for all drivers 3.4 for males 3.1 for females
500	1.8 average for all drivers 1.7 for males 2.0 females
750	1.3 average for all drivers 1.0 for males 1.8 for females

NOTE: For novice drivers, crash rates decrease dramatically from the 1st to the 7th month (41 percent), then gradually decrease through the 24th month after licensing (60 percent overall reduction) (Mayhew, Simpson, and Pak, 2003).
SOURCE: Reprinted, with permission, from McCartt et al. (2003). Copyright 2003 by Elsevier.

rates for both male and female newly licensed drivers as they accumulate miles of practice. Other research provides even more detail, showing that crash rates are highest during the first 250 miles of driving (3.2 crashes per 10,000 miles) and the second 250 miles (2.0 per 10,000 miles). After this introductory period, the crash rates decline sharply (McCartt et al., 2003).

Since few people in the United States learn to drive after their teen years, data are not available in this country to allow comparison of the experiences of younger and older novice drivers. Countries in which waiting past the teen years to begin driving is more common, such as Canada and New Zealand, have found that older novice drivers also have higher

---

a category. These adult drivers were not addressed at the workshop, but it is important to note that some proportion of teenagers have characteristics that will place them in this group once they are adults, and that the development of safe driving practices for this group may pose challenges distinct from the teen driver problem.

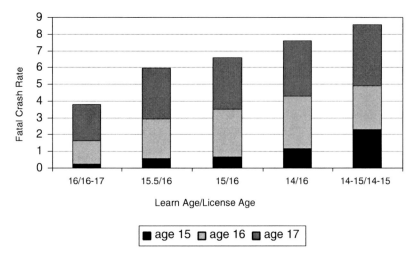

FIGURE 2-1 Driver fatal crash involvement rates (per 100,000 population, 1989-1993).
NOTE: Each column represents different groups of states, classified by the variations in ages at which practice driving (learn age) and licensure occurs, as catalogued by Williams et al., 1995.
SOURCE: Preusser (2006). Data drawn from Preusser (1995).

crash rates during their initial years of driving than do their peers with more driving experience. Nevertheless, there is evidence that even slight age differences in the adolescent years may have some effect. Figure 2-1 shows data suggesting that fatal crash rates are higher the younger the driver.

Possible reasons why waiting even 12 to 18 months beyond the once-standard 16th birthday target for licensure may be beneficial are explored in Chapter 3. However, the data on crash rates for young novice drivers are sufficiently compelling that many states have adopted graduated driver licensure (GDL) programs, which both prolong the time it takes to become fully licensed and provide for more training and supervised practice driving during the learning period. Whether the benefits come from the licensing of older adolescents, the delay itself (and consequent limitations on younger, inexperienced drivers' hours behind the wheel), or from the nature of the experiences young drivers have during the longer waiting period, these programs, which are discussed in greater detail in Chapter 4, have shown significant benefits. One study, for example, has reported an average 11 percent reduction in fatal crashes among 16-year-olds who obtained their licenses through GDL (Baker, Chen, and Guohua, 2006).

Inexperience

The newly licensed driver faces less favorable odds than does the more experienced driver, and, as Don Fisher explained, a variety of studies support the conclusion that it is newly licensed drivers' lack of experience that is the most significant problem, even considering that the youngest drivers fare the worst. For example, one analysis of police reports of almost 2,000 crashes in which newly licensed drivers were involved pointed to inexperience as the major contributor (McKnight and McKnight, 2003). These findings are consistent with those of an earlier study (Treat et al., 1979) in which ineffective visual search (scanning for hazards), speed adjustment, and attention, in that order, were implicated as causes of newly licensed driver crashes. Similarly, Gregersen (1996) estimated that some 70 percent of novice driver errors were attributable to inexperience. The errors that are typical of inexperienced drivers are discussed below.

Alcohol

Teens are especially vulnerable to the risks of drinking and driving. Younger, newly licensed drivers, as a group, have comparatively few alcohol-related crashes, while older, more experienced teen and young adult drivers have more such crashes than do adults. Nevertheless, alcohol significantly impairs driving capacity among all teenagers—and at lower blood levels than typically affect adults. As Figure 2-2 shows, the risk of crashing rises dramatically with blood alcohol content (BAC) at any age, and the effects are more marked for drivers ages 16 to 20 than for those ages 35 to 49. While peaks in substance use typically occur slightly later in the teen years (around ages 18 to 20) than driving usually begins, younger teens certainly use alcohol. Moreover, some evidence suggests that adolescents' physiological responses to alcohol may be different from those of adults, and specifically that teens may be less sensitive to signals that they are impaired (National Research Council and Institute of Medicine, 2004, 2006).

The availability of alcohol clearly poses a risk to all teen drivers.[2] A total of 24 percent of drivers ages 15 to 20 who were involved in fatal

---

[2]Not discussed at the workshop but of vital importance is the question of how underage teens obtain alcohol and ways of reducing their access to it. These topics were addressed in an earlier National Academies study on strategies to reduce underage drinking (National Research Council and Institute of Medicine, 2004).

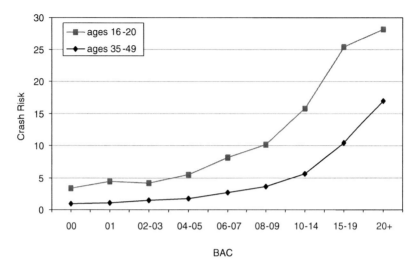

FIGURE 2-2 Crash risk by blood alcohol content (BAC).
SOURCE: Preusser (2006). Data drawn from Preusser (2002).

crashes in 2004 had a BAC of 0.08 or higher, and the percentage increased from 17 percent for 15-year-olds to 34 percent for 20-year-olds (National Highway Traffic Safety Administration, 2006b). Alcohol is much more likely to play a role in fatal crashes involving young men (26 percent) than young women (12 percent) in this age group. Crashes in which alcohol is involved tend to be more severe, and persons involved in alcohol-related crashes are less likely to be wearing seat belts. The National Highway Traffic Safety Administration (NHTSA) reports that raising the minimum legal age for drinking, which is now 21 in all states and the District of Columbia, has saved many lives—906 just in 2004. These laws are discussed more fully in Chapter 4.

Passengers

The risk of crashing is significantly elevated for teen drivers who have teenage passengers, particularly male passengers, in the car, as Anne McCartt and others made clear. Table 2-3 shows the association of passengers and the already elevated crash risk for teen drivers—the figures for 16-

TABLE 2-3 Crash Risk by Driving Alone or with Passengers, by Age of Driver

Driver Age	Alone	Passenger(s)
16	2.28	4.72
17	1.77	3.52
18	1.77	3.66
19	1.61	3.23
20-24	1.50	2.54
25-29	1.28	1.69
30-59	1.00	1.00

SOURCE: Reprinted, with permission, from Preusser et al. (1998). Copyright 2003 by Elsevier.

year-olds are particularly striking, showing a risk of 2.28 for drivers alone and 4.72 for drivers with any passengers, compared with 1.00 for drivers ages 30 to 59, with or without passengers. Additional data presented by McCartt (Table 2-4) demonstrate how the presence of multiple passengers seems to magnify the risk of crashes, whether they are caused by driver error, speeding, or alcohol consumption.

Bruce Simons-Morton offered support for the proposition that male teen passengers have a significantly larger impact on risky driving behaviors than do female passengers, although the reasons for this discrepancy are not clearly understood. Data from a study of teen driver behavior show how drivers with male passengers are likely to increase their speed and leave less distance between their own and other vehicles. Conversely, this same study indicates that the presence of female passengers frequently confers a protective effect for young drivers, both male and female.

Driving at Night

Although the majority of teen driver crashes occur during daylight hours (when teens are more likely to be on the road), fatal crash rates per miles driven are higher for teens driving at night than during the day. Nighttime conditions present significant challenges for all drivers, but the safety gap between night and day narrows significantly between age 16 and ages 30 to 40.

TABLE 2-4 Fatal Crash Characteristics, 16-Year-Old Driver Alone or with Teen Passengers (percentage)

	Driver Alone	1 Teen Passenger	2 Teen Passengers	3+ Teen Passengers
Driver error	72[a]	82	83	90
Speeding	30	45	50	59
Single vehicle	36	51	59	72
0.08+ blood alcohol level	9	8	10	12

[a]Totals may exceed 100% because crashes may involve more than one characteristic.
SOURCE: Insurance Institute for Highway Safety. Unpublished analysis of 2004 data from the Fatality Analysis Reporting System, National Highway Traffic Safety Administration.

Fatigue

Teen drivers who lack adequate sleep are also at higher risk of crashing. Fatigue can interact with other risk factors (such as speed, alcohol, and inexperience), and its role is underreported in crash data because it is not readily apparent to investigators. As a result, its relative contribution is difficult to study. Sleep deprivation may also play a role in nighttime crashes, as discussed in Chapter 3.

COMMON TEEN DRIVING ERRORS

A look at the more immediate causes of young driver crashes, among both newly licensed and more experienced drivers, provided another perspective on what can go wrong. James McKnight distinguished between the physical skills involved in operating a vehicle, which are relatively easily mastered, and the more complex capacities that are also necessary for safe driving. Recognizing and correcting for errors and detecting hazards in the roadway are key elements of driving safely, for example, and acquiring these skills takes much longer than learning the mechanics of driving. Some of the principal errors that teenagers make while driving include failure to:

• maintain attention and avoid distractions, including electronic devices in the car;

- search ahead, such as before left turns;
- search to the side, such as when yielding the right of way at an intersection;
- search to the rear, such as when changing lanes;
- adjust speed in response to traffic or road conditions;
- maintain space between their own and other vehicles, such as correct following distance;
- respond correctly to emergencies, such as recovering from a skid or sudden swerve;
- maintain basic control of the vehicle, such as keeping within a lane, braking, and turning smoothly;
- respond to traffic controls, such as traffic lights or guidance about lane use; and
- avoid driving while impaired by alcohol or sleepiness or driving a vehicle that needs repair.

McKnight offered a simplified summary of what teens need to learn to become successful drivers: *knowledge* of the rules of the road, safe operating procedures, and the consequences of not adhering to them; *understanding* that what they know and do will affect their safety; and the *skill* to control the car, handle an emergency, and recognize potential hazards in time to avoid them. As the conversation turned to intervention strategies, participants repeatedly stressed that remedies need to address these three elements in realistic ways. However, the information about risk factors and teen driver error goes only so far in explaining teen crashes—it does not address the reasons why teens often lack the critical elements. Thus, the workshop also explored the nature of adolescents and the developmental processes that they experience—with an eye to identifying ways in which this deeper knowledge could be applied to the development of more effective educational programs and prevention strategies for teen drivers.

3

Characteristics of Adolescence
That Can Affect Driving

Learning to drive is an important rite of passage, particularly in the United States, where limited public transportation in many areas can mean that the ability to drive is a key to independence. Teenagers who cannot drive may have to depend on their parents and others for mobility, and this can limit their options for employment, restrict their participation in school and community activities, and influence their social lives. Teenagers are generally eager to learn to drive—76 percent of young people age 15 or younger, for example, report that they are "very" interested in getting a license as soon as they can, David Preusser noted. Parents who may have spent many hours chauffeuring their children to and from activities may be eager for their teens to drive. But even though most teens want to drive and feel ready to handle the responsibility, a close look at their cognitive, social, and emotional development suggests that readiness to drive safely is not likely to occur automatically by the age of 16. The workshop addressed several aspects of adolescent development, with a focus on the features of this phase that are likely to have the greatest bearing on driving skills.

DEVELOPMENT—
HOW ADOLESCENTS DIFFER FROM ADULTS

A variety of affective factors influence teen decisions and behaviors, as Ronald Dahl explained. He began with what he called the health paradox of adolescence. Although adolescence is the healthiest period of the life span physically, a time when young people are close to their peak in strength, reaction time, immune function, and other health assets, their overall morbidity and mortality rates increase 200 percent from childhood to late adolescence. Many of the primary causes of death and disability in these years—which include crashes, suicide, substance abuse, and other risky behaviors—are related to problems with control of behavior and emotion.

The reasons why adolescents can have difficulty controlling their emotions and behavior are complex, and a thorough overview of decades of research on adolescent development was beyond the scope of the workshop.[1] Instead, the focus was on identifying key insights that may have particular relevance to the problem of teen crashes and to use these insights as an entry point for exploring possibilities for improving the effectiveness of teen driving safety efforts.

A complex web of physiological, psychological, and environmental conditions contributes to an increase in impulsivity in adolescents and influences both decision making and regulatory functions that affect driving as well as other adolescent behaviors. Indeed, a hallmark of this stage of life, not only in humans but also in other mammals, is the tendency toward increased risk-taking and novelty-seeking, as well as an increased focus on social context (Romer, 2003; Lerner and Steinberg, 2004). These characteristics foster the development of independence at the same time that they increase young people's exposure to risk, and it is important to note that they involve both natural and adaptive processes, even though they can have very negative results.

As might be expected, the onset of puberty plays an important role. As puberty begins, changes in the endocrine system can affect drives, motivation, mood, and emotion. This period is characterized by increased emotional intensity and changes in romantic motivation. It is associated with increases in risk-taking, novelty-seeking, and sensation-seeking, as well as an increased focus on social status. These attributes can have significant

---

[1]A comprehensive review of emerging research on adolescent development can be found in the *Handbook on Adolescent Development* edited by Lerner and Steinberg (2004). A recent report of a workshop summary from the Board on Children, Youth, and Families, *A Study of Interactions: Emerging Issues in the Science of Adolescence* (National Research Council and Institute of Medicine, 2006), also addresses some of these issues in more detail.

effects on driving behavior. Moreover, cognitive development occurs on an unrelated trajectory that is not complete until the early 20s—long after puberty is over. Thus, the capacity for planning, logical reasoning, and understanding the long-term consequences of behavior are far from fully developed during the period when most young people in America are beginning to drive.

Another key difference between adolescent and adult brains is in their capacity to manage multiple tasks at once. The capacity known as executive function, which is the key to judgment, impulse control, planning and organizing, and attention—or, as it has been called, the CEO of the brain—is situated in the prefrontal cortex, which is still under construction during the teen years. In the absence of stress and distraction, most teens function well, but this regulatory capacity can be easily overwhelmed by strong emotion, multitasking, sleep deprivation, or substance abuse (Luciana et al., 2005). The particular risks posed to teen drivers by extra passengers, music, cell phones, and other sources of stimulation or distraction begin to make sense when this aspect of teen development is understood. Other specific perspectives on adolescents offer further insight.

ADOLESCENT DECISION MAKING

Adolescents also differ in significant ways from adults in their approach to risk and decision making, as Julie Downs explained. She began by enumerating the primary factors that affect decision making in general:

- knowledge of risks,
- appreciation of the potential trade-offs between risks and benefits,
- assessment of short- and long-term expectations,
- focus on the most likely outcomes, and
- perceived alternatives to taking the risk.

The conventional wisdom about teenagers' risk-taking is that they both fail to appreciate the risks that face them and wrongly perceive themselves as invulnerable to risk in general. In fact, however, teens do not believe they are invulnerable. Their perceptions of many risks are fairly accurate, and they actually tend to rate their overall risk of premature death as far higher than it actually is. For example, while teens can estimate the likelihood of being arrested (less than 10 percent) or, among girls, becoming pregnant in the next year (6 percent) with fair accuracy, they estimate their risk of dying in the next year at 18.6 percent, while the actual risk is 0.08 percent. Teens can be overly optimistic in other areas. Nearly 73 percent, for example, predict that they will have a college degree by the age of 30, while only 30 percent actually achieve this goal.

The misperception that affects teens' driving, which they share with adults, is a tendency known as the optimistic bias, or overconfidence in their own control over risk. For example, while smokers of all ages know that smoking puts them at risk for lung disease and death, most believe their own risk is less than that of a typical smoker. What compounds this problem for teens, however, is their lack of understanding and inaccurate thinking about cumulative risk. In other words, teens correctly assess the risk associated with any single car trip as relatively low. However, each time the teen takes an uneventful drive, his or her perception of the riskiness of driving goes down while perception of the benefits goes up. While a teen driver may still acknowledge the overall risk, even after acquiring months of experience, he or she perceives a decline in the risk posed by any single driving trip. The result is a teen who believes he or she can handle hazardous situations, is overconfident of his or her driving skills, and is decreasingly vigilant about safety. Since the teen is also less experienced and competent at the wheel than the average adult, the optimistic bias is particularly hazardous for teen drivers.

THE IMPORTANT ROLE OF PEERS

Adolescents are intensely attuned to social interactions with their peers, and Sara Kinsman and Joseph Allen provided two perspectives on the key ways in which these relationships influence behavior and increase risks for young drivers and their passengers. Teens are focused on their peers for good reason, Kinsman noted, and she argued that learning to negotiate peer relationships is the most important developmental task that adolescents must accomplish. To complete the transition to adulthood, teens must learn to get along with, work with, live with, and care for their peers, and these relationships are integral to success in almost every aspect of life.

Kinsman explained that the collective process through which teens create their own culture is an important part of this task—and that it is not simply a matter of rebelling against adult norms and authority. Reciprocity is an important part of this process, so it is important for young people to demonstrate that they are a part of the collective endeavor by emphasizing ways in which they are like other members of the group. Issues of status, social groupings, and adherence to norms are all integral to this process. Because these relationships and the teen's place in his or her peer group are so important developmentally, the peer group can have as much influence on behavior as individual characteristics, such as gender, socioeconomic status, and family influences.

Peer interactions often make risky behaviors more likely. Kinsman presented data from a study by Mokdad et al. (2004), which demonstrated that teens typically initiate dangerous behaviors with peers—indeed, approximately 25 percent of all U.S. deaths are the result of activities that are initiated with peers during adolescence.

Joseph Allen amplified this point with a discussion of teens' attitudes toward deviant or risky behavior. He noted, as Ronald Dahl had as well, that teens are more prone to thrill-seeking than adults are, and that their quest to seem mature and to increase their autonomy can lead them to take risks. Rates of deviance, Allen explained, increase dramatically beginning at about age 11, peak at around age 16, and then drop off gradually over the following 10 to 15 years. Several factors combine to make all teens vulnerable to negative peer influences. Teens' great need for social acceptance combines with inexperience in handling pressure from peers. Moreover, Allen explained, popular teens are more likely than so-called average teens to engage in risky behavior at younger ages, to increase that behavior quickly, and to sustain it (Allen et al., 2005). Moreover, as Kinsman noted, popular teens are socially adept and have a skill set different from that of others. They have a particularly strong influence on youngsters who are social followers—eager to improve their social status by association with more popular peers. Thus, in many cases, the teens in leadership positions are more likely to instigate risky behavior—but teens who are struggling socially may be more susceptible to negative influences.

Driving—the single activity that involves the greatest risks for the largest number of teens—can play an important role in peer interactions. The ability to drive one's friends around can allow teens to pursue important social goals, for example, by allowing them to demonstrate maturity, return favors that others have offered, enhance their status, reinforce membership in a group, or host the social event that a group car trip can be. The key point in terms of driving safety is that when driving with peers, teens are undertaking two separate, challenging, and complex tasks: they are keenly attuned to the behavior of and interactions among their peers while also operating the vehicle and attending to road and traffic conditions. From a developmental perspective, Kinsman argued, it is unrealistic to expect teens to tune out their peer passengers and give their full attention to the task of driving.

Allen described the situation in a car full of teenagers as "the perfect storm," because four elements come together in that situation: peers who may value risky behavior, teens who need social acceptance, the likelihood that the riskiest teens will be the loudest, and all teens' relative lack of immunity to peer pressure. At the same time, the teen who is driving cannot easily see the faces of the passengers, which increases the stress of staying attuned to the social dynamics, yet it is the driver who is primarily responsible for the safety of the situation.

Allen argued that it may be possible to harness peer influences in positive ways if strategies can be found to link responsible driving with attributes or rewards that teens value. For example, teens value both self-confidence and skill, and they also value money and material goods. Thus, a program that took these values into account by offering rewards for demonstrating responsible driving skills in specific ways—such as driving for a certain period without any violations or passing a series of tests—would have the benefit of meeting teens on their own terms.

SLEEP DEPRIVATION

Another way in which teens differ from adults is in their need for sleep—and in the factors that work against their getting enough sleep. Alertness is key to safe driving at any age, and adequate sleep is an important contributor to alertness and the capacity to focus on all the details a safe driver must monitor. Adolescents are chronically short on sleep, as Mary Carskadon explained, and the result is more crashes in this age group. Figure 3-1 shows the age distribution for crashes caused by drivers who fell asleep at the wheel, with a sharp peak in the teenage years.

High school students need approximately 9 hours of sleep per night, but generally get between 7 and 7.5 hours. College students also get more than an hour less per night than the 8.4 hours they need. Both biological factors and the circumstances of young people's lives play a role in this chronic sleep deficit. During the adolescent years, young people's sleep needs increase and their circadian (sleeping and waking) rhythms also change. The net result is that teenagers have a biologically driven tendency to stay up later at night and sleep longer in the morning, at the same time that their daily sleep requirements increase over what was needed in late childhood.

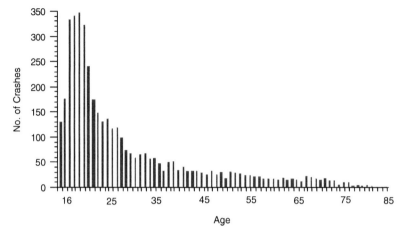

FIGURE 3-1 Age distribution of drivers in fall-asleep crashes.
SOURCE: Reprinted, with permission, from Pack et al., 1995. Copyright 1995 by Elsevier.

While these processes are taking place, other factors are working against sleep for many teens. In the same period when parents are gradually relinquishing control over teens' daily lives, particularly bedtime and other daily functions, both academic obligations and social opportunities are generally increasing—and giving teens reasons to stay up at night. Moreover, a 2006 National Sleep Foundation study found that 97 percent of adolescents have at least one electronic device in their bedroom (e.g., television, computer, Internet access, cell phone, music player), so the array of stimulating activities that might keep them awake is far more diverse than it was a generation ago (National Sleep Foundation, 2006). The same study showed that the presence of four or more electronic devices in the bedroom is associated with a loss of 30 minutes of sleep per day, on average.

Adolescents stay up too late, but they are also required to wake up quite early for school. School bus schedules as well as pressure to end the school day in time for after-school sports practices and other activities have generally caused school officials to set early start times for high schools. Many communities have attempted to address the tension between these pressures and adolescents' natural impulse to sleep later in the morning. Some have adopted later start times, and efforts to make this change are ongoing in many communities. However, with many teens staying up until midnight and well beyond, an extra 30 to 60 minutes of sleep in the morn-ing—all that most communities have been able to muster—may not be enough to address the problem.

The effects of sleepiness on driving are striking. After 17 hours awake (for example, a teen who woke up at 6:30 a.m. and is still socializing at 11:30 p.m.), a teen's performance is impaired to the same extent that it would be with a blood alcohol content of 0.05 percent. Driving home from the prom at 6:30 in the morning (after 24 hours awake), a teen's driving would be impaired as much as it would be with a blood alcohol content of 0.10 percent. Apart from late-night driving and unusual circumstances that cause extensive sleep deprivation, teens are at their sleepiest in the morning, and the rate of fall-asleep crashes for 16- to 25-year-olds confirms this, peaking between 6 and 8 in the morning (Pack et al., 1995).

The bottom line, Carskadon concluded, is that many adolescents and young adults are not getting sufficient sleep to meet the needs of their growing bodies, with the result that they are at increased risk of crashing when they drive.

THE SOCIAL CONTEXT OF TEEN DRIVING

The cognitive and social development that takes place during adoles-cence interacts with individual personality traits, driving experience and ability, characteristics of the vehicle, and the roadway environment to in-fluence driving behavior and safety, as Susan Ferguson pointed out. Other individual factors may be particularly relevant to driving as well. David Preusser noted that there is a body of literature dating back to the 1960s on the relationships between juvenile delinquency, dropping out of school, and poor academic achievement, as well as socioeconomic factors, family structure, and risk behaviors in adolescence and crashes (Preusser, 1995).

This initial sketch of key characteristics of adolescence points to pros-pects for significantly improving driving safety for teens by building inter-ventions that draw on the relevance of the social context of teen driving and the cognitive and social development processes that occur during these years. Moreover, most of the attention in research on traffic safety has fo-cused on risk factors, but adolescents also have many characteristics that can work in support of safety. Prevention strategies developed in other pub-lic health contexts that draw on young people's many strengths may well be applicable to the problem of teen crashes.

The extent to which the characteristics of adolescents and their developmental processes are not adequately taken into account in driver's education, licensing, and supervisory practices for young drivers was a persistent theme throughout the workshop. The next chapter explores current and potential strategies that might contribute to prevention efforts.

4

Strategies to Improve Safety

Policies, laws, and other strategies can clearly affect teens' driving behavior and their safety. Data presented on the effects of graduated driver licensing and minimum drinking age laws, for example, demonstrate that injury and fatality rates are not immutable, despite the fact that, as Robert Foss pointed out, human beings are difficult to change. This chapter first describes strategies already in place and then explores additional strategies, such as greater parental engagement in supervising teen drivers, that offer potential to significantly increase safe driving behaviors among teens.

CURRENT STRATEGIES

At present, two key tools are used to improve the safety of teen drivers: driver education and the legal structure of testing and licensure.

Driver Education

Driver education programs, first developed in the 1930s, became increasingly widespread in the United States between the 1940s and the 1970s, according to Richard Compton, who provided an overview of the history of this crash prevention strategy, research on its effectiveness, and current trends. A basic model of 30 hours of classroom instruction, often given at public high schools, plus six hours of instruction behind the wheel of a car was established in most states. In the intervening decades, however, these programs did not reduce crash involvement among beginning drivers. Recognizing that no differences emerged in the crash records of driver education graduates and those of equivalent groups of beginning drivers who learned to drive without formal education, many states scaled back funding for these programs. From a peak in 1976, when 3,200,000 students in 17,000 public schools took driver education courses, the number has steadily declined. In 1981 the National Highway Traffic Safety Administration (NHTSA) dropped driver education from its list of priority programs; however, many states still require formal training as a condition of licensure prior to age 18.

The goals for driver education classes are generally straightforward— to teach young people the rules of the road, the basic skills they need to control the car, and safe driving practices, such as defensive driving and risk assessment. Research conducted during the early years (1940 through 1960) generally yielded the positive finding that the programs produced safer drivers. Later researchers, however, cast doubt on the findings of earlier studies, finding that their methodology did not take into account significant differences between those who did and did not take the courses, for example. Such differences might include individual motivations and safety mindedness, as well as larger demographic differences related to socioeconomic status. Moreover, newer studies indicated that the availability of driver education programs (in states that require teens who wish to be licensed before age 18 to successfully complete such a program) provided the opportunity for young people to get a license before age 18. When more drivers under 18 are licensed, more teens are at risk of crashing and more crashes occur.[1] Finally, a large-scale 1983 NHTSA state-of-the-art study (the "DeKalb study") (Stock et al., 1983) used randomized assignment to evaluate the impact of the driver education curriculum, and the results did not support the effectiveness of driver education in reducing crash rates. In response to that study, governmental support for driver education declined (Mayhew and Simpson, 1997; Young, 1993).

Driver education is not viewed as a lost cause by safety experts, however. Suggestions have been made that these programs could address safety

---

[1]It should be noted that the 1960s legislative requirements that teens complete driver education by age 18 had the effect of delaying licensure.

skills in new ways, by addressing teens' tendency toward risk-taking and overconfidence and by increasing parental involvement, for example. Workshop participants emphasized the importance of introducing driver education within a broader framework of graduated licensing, making distinctions between developing the manual skills that are necessary to operate a complex vehicle and acquiring the expertise and judgment to recognize hazards and to exercise caution when driving under risky conditions. While traditional programs tend to emphasize the former, the latter area remains unaddressed in the curricula of many driver education programs. In exploring the merits of driver education, Compton noted that NHTSA is reviewing opportunities for improvement and is considering new curriculum guidelines as well as standards for teachers. In addition, NHTSA is developing a national and international review to identify instructional tools, training methods, and curricula that are consistent with best practices in selected states and other countries.

A related issue is the relatively recent development of private courses that focus on enhancing driving skills in hazardous conditions. Often taught by former race car drivers or others with experience in "extreme" driving, these courses may use technology to simulate such hazards as slippery roads, or they may present teens with actual hazards in safe settings, and allow teens to learn skills for handling them. While these programs are appealing to many parents, few data are available to demonstrate their effectiveness. Indeed, a few studies have shown that the crash rate for young drivers, especially young men, who receive skid training is higher than for those who do not (Jones, 1993; Glad, 1988). Several participants mentioned that taking such a course might actually foster overconfidence in some teens, who might demonstrate show-off behavior and exercise less caution because they believe their new skills will allow them to handle any hazard (Williams, 2006). On one hand, this concern is consistent with the recognition that teens may seek out novel opportunities to try out new skills—or they may perceive that they have more control over the vehicle than they really do—thus increasing their exposure to crashes. On the other hand, experience with certain types of hazards may be of real benefit to many teens. Continued use of similar programs to train police officers and other adults who need these skills suggests that some aspects of these programs merit further exploration to determine their potential benefits for teen drivers.

Licensure and the Law

Driver education, regardless of its content, has not been mandatory for all teens, but state laws affect all teens who want to drive legally. Anne McCartt provided an overview of legal and regulatory approaches to reducing teen crashes and indicated that strong laws, combined with well publicized enforcement, have been the most effective measures in changing teen drivers' behavior.

One target of state law has been driving under the influence of alcohol. As McCartt explained, teens are actually somewhat less likely than adults to drive while impaired by alcohol, but their crash risk is greater when they do so, particularly when their blood alcohol content (BAC) is low or moderate. To combat this problem, all U.S. states have now made the minimum legal drinking age 21, and all have adopted "zero tolerance" laws that prohibit teens from driving with a level of alcohol above 0.02 percent in their systems. These laws have significantly reduced the rates of fatally injured drivers ages 16 to 19. For example, the percentage of fatally injured drivers with BACs of 0.08 percent or higher has fallen from 51 percent in 1982 to 23 percent in 2003. However, McCartt noted that progress has stalled in recent years, and she argued that increased enforcement is needed to further reduce alcohol-related teen crashes.[2]

The other major strategy that states have increasingly adopted involves changes in testing and licensure for new drivers. Standard testing for a license to operate a motor vehicle assesses knowledge of traffic safety rules and operation of the vehicle. Students may prepare for the written and road tests by memorizing information about speed limits and traffic rules and by practicing parking or navigating intersections. The tests generally do not assess the capacity to handle more complex scenarios, nor do they require students to identify potential hazards or to address unexpected circumstances, distractions, or peer pressures that are common features of normal driving conditions.

Recognizing the high risks teens face in their first months on the road and the important opportunity that testing and licensure offer to shape

---

[2]Law enforcement, parental influence, and social marketing messages are all strategies for addressing teens' access to alcohol (National Research Council and Institute of Medicine, 2004).

their driving behavior, many states have adopted some version of graduated driver licensing (GDL). As the name implies, GDL is a means of slowing down the process of obtaining the license, controlling the circumstances under which teens drive while they are learning, and thus increasing their exposure to higher risk conditions (such as nighttime driving and driving with teen passengers) in a gradual, controlled way.

Typically, the GDL process has three phases—an extended supervised practice stage for teens possessing learner's permits, a provisional licensure stage during which restrictions are imposed, and then full licensure. Many states have adopted specific practice requirements for the first phase, such as 30 or 40 hours of supervised driving, to supplement any driver education classes teens might take. The provisional license stage includes restrictions on teen exposure to circumstances that are known risk factors.

A significant number of states have adopted elements of GDL in the past 10 years (Table 4-1), and many states continue to update their requirements to include additional features.

As Allan Williams noted, however, no single state has adopted all of the features of GDL that are viewed as constituting best practice. On one hand, in some states, parents or other groups have successfully resisted efforts to implement GDL provisions, opposing proposals to extend the supervisory period for newly licensed youth. On the other hand, smaller numbers of states have more recently increased restrictions on night driving and carrying passengers, increased requirements for supervised driving, or banned the use of cell phones while driving.

The benefits of GDL are clear, as McCartt and others emphasized. The combination of limiting driving in hazardous situations, increasing the amount of supervised practice driving, and delaying full licensure seems

TABLE 4-1 State Adoption of Licensing Requirements

	1995	2006
Minimum learner's permit age 16 or older	8 states	9 states
Learner's permit for at least 6 months	0	42
30 or more hours of certified driving	0	30
Night driving restriction once licensed	9	45
Passenger restriction once licensed	0	36

SOURCE: Reprinted, with permission, from Insurance Institute for Highway Safety (2006).

TABLE 4-2 Evaluations of Graduated Licensing Programs in the United States

	Age Group	Crash Reduction Rate (%)
California	15-17	0
California	16	17
California	16-17	28
Florida	15-17	9
Michigan	16	29
North Carolina	16	34
Ohio	16-17	23
Wisconsin	16	14

SOURCES: California ages 15-17: Masten and Hagge (2004); California age 16: Cooper et al. (2004); California ages 16-17: Rice et al. (2004); Florida: Ulmer et al. (2000); Michigan: Shope and Molnar (2004); North Carolina: unpublished data, available from Rob Foss at Highway Safety Research Center; Ohio: Ohio Department of Public Safety (2001); Wisconsin: Fohr et al. (2005).

to target key risk factors associated with teen driving. One study has shown an 11 percent decrease in fatal crashes among 16-year-olds in states that have some form of GDL, with larger decreases occurring in states that have the most comprehensive programs (Baker, Chen, and Guohua, 2006). Evaluations cited by McCartt showed marked reductions in crash rates for 16- and 17-year-olds following the adoption of GDL in several states (Table 4-2).

As with the drinking laws, however, McCartt and others noted that GDL programs would be more effective if enforcement—both by parents and law enforcement officials—was tougher. GDL in particular depends on parents to enforce many of its provisions, both to supervise their children for the required number of driving hours and to monitor their adherence to passenger and night-driving restrictions. Moreover, while the value of traditional driver education has come into question, ways to improve it and link it to GDL provisions have not yet become a primary focus for states.

Several participants mentioned the broader role of law enforcement policies, the potential impact of teens' perception that laws are being enforced, and the role of the insurance industry as areas that deserved further attention in the development of prevention strategies to reduce teen crashes.

The time allotted for the workshop did not provide opportunity to adequately address the potential for these groups to contribute to proactive improvements in safety. Other strategies with potential were addressed in greater detail and are described below.

STRATEGIES WITH POTENTIAL

While GDL and minimum drinking age laws have led to reductions in risky driving and crashes, teen crash rates remain unacceptably high. Persistent concern about the issue is now stimulating a search to identify existing strategies that are not being exploited to their full potential. In addition, new technical interventions now offer the potential to protect novice drivers—and all drivers—in previously unimaginable ways.

Parents

The success of GDL has focused attention on the role that parents can and must play in the critical learning period for teen drivers. As Bruce Simons-Morton explained, parents influence teens' actions during this period in a variety of ways, for good or ill; their intentions are good but the outcome is mixed. Parenting practices, parents' knowledge, and the relationship between parents and their children all contribute to teenagers' acquiring safe driving practices. Parents can play a critical role, but in many cases they don't know what they should be doing to help their children drive safely—or how best to do it. Moreover, policy makers and others frequently do not take advantage of the opportunities they have to help parents become effective driving coaches and supervisors while their children are novice drivers.

Taking the parent-teen relationship first, Simons-Morton called attention to the familiar model of authoritative parenting that psychologists advocate, in which parents make and enforce rules but also are supportive, flexible, and responsive to their teens. If parents are involved in their children's lives, monitor their children's behavior, convey their expectations clearly, impose consequences, and maintain open communication and a sense of mutual trust, outcomes are likely to be better than if they do not.

However, even when these conditions are all in place, a variety of factors pushes both teens and parents to favor driving privileges. Parents as well as teens can be naïve about the actual risks of crashing. Parents may be satisfied with the teen's mastery of the mechanical skills of managing the vehicle and fail to appreciate the importance of other safe driving skills, such as hazard detection, risk assessment, and anticipatory behaviors. Both parents and teens are subject to social pressures in favor of teen driving, and at the same time, parents may be eager to stop driving their teens around. Teens are generally eager to drive, and parents want to give them the gift of independence.

Simons-Morton summarized the more specific ways in which parents can influence teen driving and their potential effects on safety. Two things they can do have demonstrated safety benefits: delaying permission to test for a driving license and controlling access to the vehicles and driving circumstances (such as night driving and carrying passengers) for novice drivers. When it comes to drinking and driving, the role of parents is complex, and Simons-Morton noted that the example parents set may far outweigh other messages they attempt to send. Moreover, parents may believe they have explained what their children should do if they find themselves in a situation that involves drinking and driving, but teens report that they are not sure.

Finally, supervised practice driving, required in increasing numbers of state GDL programs, has significant potential, but it has not yet demonstrated safety effects (such as changes in crash or mortality rates) on its own in the United States, perhaps because parents have been offered little guidance on how to make use of this time. Another issue with supervised driving is that when parents are in the car, they tend to have the primary responsibility for safety and risk assessment, even if the teen is driving. They are scanning for hazards, coaching and guiding the teen, and may be making or influencing many of the decisions about acceptable conditions, avoiding dangerous intersections, and so forth. Thus, once the teen drives alone, the initial period of practice driving has not necessarily prepared him or her to anticipate hazards. There is a need to identify specific components of supervised driving, Simons-Morton explained, that can be tested experimentally and are associated with increased knowledge and behavioral improvements among youth. Developing driving proficiency requires experience, so the key is to allow learning drivers to gain that experience in circumstances that are relatively safe. Figure 4-1 compares crash rates for novice drivers who do and do not learn under supervised circumstances.

A program called Checkpoints, developed by researchers at the National Institute of Child Health and Human Development, provides a structure in which parents can work with their teens to reduce risk conditions during the first 12 months of driving. The program uses a combination of

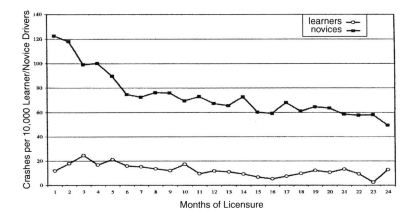

FIGURE 4-1 Crash rates by license status and months of licensure.
SOURCE: Reprinted, with permission, from McCartt, Shabanova, and Leaf (2003).
Copyright 2003 by Elsevier.

tools, including persuasive communications, such as videos and newsletters, written agreements between parents and their children, and limits on high-risk driving privileges. A controlled study, in which some families participated in the Checkpoints program and others received comparable driving safety materials but not all of the Checkpoints interventions, showed that Checkpoints families imposed and maintained significantly more restrictions on their teenagers' driving. However, the study sample was not large enough to show ultimate effects on crash rates.

The Checkpoints program is based on the goals of changing both parents' and teens' perception of their risk, as well as their expectations regarding reasonable limitations—in order to decrease risky driving, traffic violations, and crashes. Although initial results for Checkpoints are positive, Simons-Morton noted, additional research on changes in novice driving performance over the first 18 months of driving, on the nature and effects of supervised driving, on other ways to deliver support and improve parental management, and on ways to incorporate findings about the process of learning to drive into driver education and testing and licensure programs would be of great benefit.

Richard Catalano provided an additional perspective on the role of family influences with a framework that is part of a larger social development approach to risk prevention. Key risk and protective factors that affect adolescent behavior may be evident long before youngsters reach the teen years, he explained, and targeted strategies can be used to improve outcomes for teens. Catalano described a study called Raising Healthy Children (RHC), in which five matched pairs of elementary schools were randomly assigned to receive either a prevention program based on the social development approach or a control condition.

The risk and protective factors addressed in the RHC program are listed in Box 4-1. Such interventions as teacher and parent workshops, in-home services, and summer and after-school programs were offered to children as young as first grade to focus on such goals as developing social and other skills, addressing school and family management problems, and promoting prosocial behaviors. Brief family sessions were offered to families at critical transition points, including the transition from middle to high school, the transition out of high school, and the transition to driving.

BOX 4-1
Risk and Protective Factors

Risk Factors
- School
  - Low commitment to school
  - Academic failure
- Family
  - Poor family management
  - Family conflict
  - Favorable parental attitudes and involvement in the problem behavior
- Individual and Peer
  - Early antisocial behavior
  - Favorable attitudes
  - Early initiation
  - Friends who engage in problem behaviors
  - Constitutional factors

Protective Factors
- In the socializing units of family, school, and peers:
  - Opportunities
  - Skills
  - Recognition
  - Bonding
  - Healthy beliefs and clear standards

Based on the proposition that good parenting reduces poor driving, the sessions designed to improve driving safety had specific objectives. In the first session, parents and teens discuss trying new things in adolescence and examine their perspectives on risk-taking. In this discussion, parents and teens seek to understand the current driving laws and the risks of driving while young and inexperienced. In addition, teens practice skills for making healthy choices, focusing on motivations and consequences, while parents demonstrate the ability to coach their teen in using decision-making skills to reduce conflict and to establish effective communication. The session concludes with an exercise in which parents and teens strive to integrate this information and skills into guidelines and expectations for driving.

The second session had four goals:

(1)   parents display competence in using communication and anger management skills with their teen;

(2)   teens learn how to handle crashes, dead batteries, flat tires;

(3)   parents and teens implement a family driving contract; and

(4)   parents and teens apply a "guidelines, monitoring, and consequences" approach to driving-related difficulties and conflict (demonstrate knowledge and use of effective consequences, identify ideas for recognizing teens' positive driving behavior).

Bearing in mind that the program was designed to address a broader range of risks than just those associated with driving, the program has demonstrated some promising results. For example, families receiving the intervention were four to six times more likely than the control families to report that they had established a driving contract. Teens in the families receiving the intervention also reported that they drove less frequently under the influence of alcohol or rode with peers who had been drinking.

While participants agreed that more study of effective means to harness the potential of parents and family dynamics in improving teens' driving safety is needed, the potential benefits seemed clear.

Health Care Providers

Health care providers are not all doing their part to provide prevention messages to adolescents and their parents, according to specialist in adolescent and young adult medicine Lawrence D'Angelo. He indicated that this gap is notable, especially in light of evidence that this kind of counseling has had positive effects in other areas, such as reducing smoking. Driving safety is not a prominent topic during medical students' training in pediatrics, he explained. Consequently, even experts in adolescent medicine (who receive specialized training and certification) report providing counseling about alcohol, drugs, and/or automobiles only 82.5 percent of the time during their annual examinations of adolescent patients. Specific threats to adolescent health, such as the risks of having passengers in the car and night driving, are mentioned far less frequently (12 and 7 percent, respectively). Indeed, D'Angelo pointed out, only 60 percent of adolescent specialists know whether the state has a GDL law, and the percentage was only slightly higher among those with adolescents in their own household (77 percent).

Another health care-based strategy that has not been well explored, participants pointed out, is that of pursuing individual characteristics that may increase driving risk. Attention deficit hyperactivity disorder, type 1 diabetes, and substance abuse are just a few of the factors that might put an individual teen at increased risk when driving. Teens with these problems are not routinely counseled about how their diagnoses may affect driving. Yet patients with other health risk factors, such as those for cardiovascular disease, are routinely identified and patients are counseled on ways to minimize negative outcomes.

Guidelines for health care providers, innovative ways of delivering counseling to youth and their families, and additional research that encompasses a broader health agenda for adolescents were all mentioned as viable ways to encourage providers to address teen driving risks. The role of public health agencies in addressing the risks of teen driving, as well as opportunities to promote responsible driving practices, were identified as particularly deserving further attention.

Technology

Without a doubt, intensified and improved efforts using existing strategies could yield further improvements in safety, but they offer only partial solutions to the fundamental problem—allowing young people to learn driving skills and gain experience behind the wheel without risking their lives. Many of the strategies already discussed address ways in which adults might either persuade or compel teens to behave differently or improve the training they receive or the quality of their practice time behind the wheel.

Technology offers a very powerful companion strategy with significant potential to make driving safer not just for novices but for all drivers. Max Donath, Wade Allen, and John Lee described some of the technological innovations with particular promise.

Technology in the Car

Donath began by noting a few reasons why technology offers significant opportunities to reduce crash and fatality rates. Measures to increase seat belt use, for example, have had a significant impact on survival rates, but this improvement increased markedly as the policies shifted from voluntary interventions to mandatory requirements. When seat belts were first introduced in large numbers of cars in the 1960s, for example, they were used less than 25 percent of the time, and they were generally used by the lowest risk drivers. State laws requiring the use of seat belts helped to boost implementation rates, but large proportions of the driving population who were at higher risk of crash involvement did not tend to use the safety restraints until enforcement provisions were legally mandated. At present, teenage boys continue to be one of the groups least likely to wear seat belts (Transportation Research Board, 1989, 2003).

Other, more complex technologies can influence other driving behaviors, Donath noted, in one of three ways.

The first is *forcing behavior*, which involves using technology to make it impossible to operate the vehicle in certain circumstances. For example, a seat belt interlock can prevent the car from starting unless all occupants have engaged their seat belts. An alcohol ignition interlock feature requires the driver to puff into a tube connected to a BAC sensor, which engages the interlock if a preset BAC threshold is breached. Intelligent speed adaptation (ISA), in which a system using a global positioning system (GPS) and a digital road map can prevent a driver from exceeding the posted speed limit, is another example of forcing behavior. ISA may also use the second of the three approaches, driver feedback, by signaling to the driver the need to reduce speed. Some versions of ISA are even designed to adapt warnings to such factors as road and weather conditions, traffic congestion, and time of day. Interlock systems can be installed when cars are manufactured, so new vehicles might come with "smart" keys that identify drivers, for example, with the possibility of programming different restrictions for different members of a family.

Driver feedback is a system for providing real-time warnings of poor driving, hazardous conditions, or other potential risks. For example, this technology might recognize curves in the road or departure from a lane and alert the driver to make corrections to speed and steering. This type of technology could also be used to control misuse of entertainment systems, which can be very distracting for teen (and other) drivers.

Reporting behavior is a system for collecting data about driver performance that can either be saved for later review by parents or other driving supervisors or transmitted in real time so that parents have the option to intervene. The driving "report card" might include data on speed, acceleration, braking, throttle use, and time and location of the trip, which can allow parents to supervise their teen's driving even when they are not physically present. Such programs may be initiated through novel features, such as cell phones or web sites that use GPS to report phone or vehicle location, speed and direction of travel, and time of day on a routine basis.[3]

John Lee described other kinds of driver supports that can enhance safety, some of which are already available and some of which will be soon. Forward collision warnings, road departure warnings, and steering assist devices are among the adaptive technologies that can either warn the driver of a potential risk or actually intervene to minimize or prevent it. He predicted that the market for such devices could reach $10 to $100 billion by 2010.

While many technical innovations offer promising approaches to prevention, several participants observed that new interventions and technology need to be carefully evaluated before they are widely adopted. Eagerness to reduce teen driver crashes can too easily encourage the adoption of new devices based on a perception of potential benefits rather than a rigorous assessment of their actual effects and risks. Although some technical innovations may offer superior ways to teach driving skills and prevent some impaired drivers from operating their vehicles, the overall effects of technology on changing attitudes among the youth population about risk and responsible driving may be very small. Drivers may also adapt to new technologies in unexpected ways, taking other risks that lessen the intended value of the new devices. In addition, public resistance to forced behaviors or technical overrides should not be underestimated.

---

[3]One device that can be used for both reporting and feedback is the so-called black box, which collects a variety of data and is now standard in most new vehicles sold in the United States. Currently, black box data are generally not made available to researchers or licensing authorities in the United States, but they could provide useful insights into the precursors of crashes.

Technology in Driver Education

As discussed above, traditional driver education has focused on teaching skills, driving practices, and the rules of the road. Computer-based instruction makes it possible for the objectives of driver education to include not only a more complex conception of driving skills—encompassing perceptual, psychomotor, and cognitive skills—but also attitudes about driving and risk-taking and a wider range of knowledge about the challenges of driving. As Wade Allen, who provided an overview of the potential of this technology, explained, computer-based instruction also offers practical advantages as well—it can be administered on the web, for example, and can be provided consistently and easily by school districts and driver education schools.

The primary advantage of computer-based instruction is that it can use scoring to motivate and encourage students and to focus attention on the criteria for successful completion of the course. As it does in other contexts, computer-based instruction allows novice drivers to practice handling hazardous situations without risking their lives. Students can experience roadway and traffic hazards, even crashes, in real time and practice situational awareness (awareness of the surrounding situation and potential risks) and decision making under stress. Scoring for practice sessions can instantly indicate the consequences of driver decisions. Computer adaptive technology could allow the program to focus on a student's weaknesses, allowing follow-up practice to reinforce learning from mistakes.

Computer-based instruction can be delivered on a desktop computer (the least expensive model), in a console simulator or a more complex display system, or by means of a portable computer installed in a vehicle that is equipped with a virtual reality headset (the car's wheels are placed on turntables so the learner can operate the steering wheel). Although the costs increase significantly with the complexity of the hardware, the face validity—that is, the extent to which the simulated experience resembles a real-life experience—is likely to correspond to the sophistication of the hardware as well.

As Allen explained, the benefits of computer-based instruction are many and the obstacles to widespread adoption are not technological but economic and social. This point hearkens back to earlier discussion of strategies that are underused, as well as to a broader point that emerged throughout the workshop sessions: a broad, multifaceted approach offers the greatest potential to bring about meaningful improvements in driving safety for teens.

5

Moving Forward

The workshop demonstrated that a wealth of information is available that can be used to save lives and reduce injuries from teen driving—from statistics that fill out the picture of how teenagers are harmed in crashes, to insights about how their physical, cognitive, and emotional development affects their behavior, to cutting-edge technology for making vehicles safer and improving training. As participants sifted through this material, two key points emerged. First, using this wealth of information to reduce the number of teens killed in crashes requires purposeful coordination among a variety of actors, and, second, several important questions still require research.

NEED FOR SYNTHESIS, COORDINATION, AND APPLICATION

Daniel Keating noted that each of the discussions, whether focused on aspects of adolescent development, the errors teen drivers make, or strategies for improving safety, referred frequently to omissions in skills and judgment. For him, the stark data showing the drop-off in crash rates after the first few months or few hundred miles on the road suggests the relevance of a growing body of knowledge from cognitive psychology on the development of expertise, which he emphasized is different from the simpler acquisition of skills or experience.

Keating offered a brief overview of the way expertise develops, noting that it takes considerable time in almost any context. True expertise entails not only the development of particular sets of physical skills, but also the development of judgment about how and when to apply particular skills and knowledge. Essential to the process, again regardless of the context, is learning from errors. Errors made while learning to drive can be fatal, but Keating offered the example of the Ache people of eastern Paraguay, who have addressed the risks inherent in learning to hunt in a way strikingly similar to graduated driver licensing (GDL). In that tribe, at approximately age 13, youngsters begin to learn to hunt, but they are allowed to track only certain kinds of game. The process of learning encompasses several levels of increasing difficulty and risk, and it culminates in a status akin to full certification as hunter.

Keating observed that some studies indicate that it can take up to 10,000 hours of focused, goal-directed effort to develop real expertise in acquiring a complex, modern skill. He linked the processes that are necessary to develop expertise to the development of self-regulation in adolescents. Critical to the capacity to develop and successfully deploy the judgment and skills that come with growing expertise is the capacity to regulate one's attention, emotions, and social behavior, which is still developing in teenagers. The relevance of each of these domains to driving is clear, but no purposeful strategy is available to address them in preparing young drivers. Moreover, Keating explained, it is the development of the prefrontal cortex in the brain during adolescence that regulates these capacities. During adolescence the prefrontal system emerges as the governor of other brain systems. Neural pathways, partly dictated by experience, are established in the brain that will influence development and behavior—thus providing the basis for a lifetime of safe driving habits.

In related work, some researchers have pointed out that adolescence is a period during which the basic neural pathways are established for accomplishing complex tasks through the formation of representational, psychological, and neural models that allow them to capture the "gist" of the task without requiring them to consciously decide each component of a complex endeavor each and every time. The frequent rehearsal of these tasks allows for greater speed in their execution and also allows the models to become embedded in the brain's architecture and chemistry so that the execution of repetitive tasks (such as acceleration and braking) becomes automatic. It is during the formative period of the representational model and neural circuitry that prevention strategies, hazard assessment skills, and safe driving practices acquire special significance.

The significance of these points for teen driving is twofold, Keating explained. First, they demonstrate the importance of what he called evidence-based advocacy. While policy makers may not need to delve into the intricacies of brain development in adolescence, it is important that advocates recognize and use the full range of knowledge that supports the push for a strategy such as GDL. No one at the workshop dissented from the view, mentioned numerous times, that there is no good reason to license young people to drive at age 16. But gaining support for further restraints or delays on what is commonly accepted as a natural rite of passage for adolescence would require a crisp summary of the implications of the developmental status of youngsters at this stage for driving and an evidence base that could demonstrate the costs and benefits associated with different ages of licensure. Even with 18-year-olds, the crash rates in the first few months following licensure are very high. The work of pulling together this kind of knowledge from the behavioral and social sciences and considering its practical application to driver education and other tools is only just beginning.

James Hedlund amplified this point when he described an ideal comprehensive approach to safe teen driving. Such a system would include:

• driver education that uses computer technology and is integrated with a strict GDL program;
• departments of motor vehicles that implement and enforce comprehensive GDL programs and modern methods of testing for licensure that address the range of skills that teens need to develop;
• supports for parents that guide them in managing their teens' driving and supervising their practice driving hours;
• law enforcement that makes sure teens recognize that laws and restrictions will be enforced; and
• a comprehensive community health program for driving safety that links health care practitioners, public health messages, and data collection strategies.

This list illustrates a point that was made repeatedly: not only must a wide range of knowledge be incorporated into thinking about ways to keep teens safe when they drive, but also new opportunities are needed for a range of individuals and groups to collaborate to apply this complex set of knowledge in consistent, effective ways. Possibilities include: in-depth reviews of the research literature, such as those conducted in the course of ad hoc consensus studies by the National Academies or occasional workshops, roundtables, or forums on topics of common interest. The critical need is for researchers, policy makers, advocates, and stakeholders to have sustained opportunities for dialogue and the critical examination of emerging research and strategies to apply this knowledge both to public policy and to the development of new prevention programs. Such gatherings could also stimulate the development of new public- and private-sector partnerships that would build on and strengthen existing prevention efforts, fostering consensus about innovative strategies. Although the success of GDL and other measures demonstrates the possibilities for further reducing crash rates, the synthesis and collaboration that are needed to move forward will not happen automatically.

SPECIFIC RESEARCH NEEDS

Despite the significant research findings and promising strategies that were highlighted at the workshop, participants identified a number of gaps in the existing research base. Members of the workshop committee drew on the full discussion to generate a list of key questions to guide future efforts.

What happens during the first few months of driving? What, exactly, changes and how does this change occur in different age groups? Both further insight into crashes that involve newly licensed drivers and identification of the essential skills that driver education should instill in novice drivers are needed. How can minor driving mishaps or near misses be used as teachable moments? What can be learned from naturalistic studies of teen driving behavior? What are the characteristics of adolescents who drive safely from the start? What cognitive, sensory, or behavioral factors might influence the formation of safety driving practices and stimulate the development of expertise in this realm?

What are the benefits and possible risks of new technologies? Can technology be used in more individualized ways, for example to track driver progress over time and to provide feedback that strengthens error correction and hazard detection? Can technologies such as global positioning systems provide more insight into the environmental conditions and settings that foster risky behaviors or encourage safer driving practices? Could some technologies have unforeseen negative consequences, such as preventing learning drivers from developing certain skills by superseding their judgment?

What are the best ways to influence parents' behavior? What can be done to support parents and other adults in guiding and supervising their teens and also to increase parents' motivation to monitor and restrict their teens? How might adolescents' health care providers be coached to increase their counselling on driving safety and the effectiveness of their efforts?

What are the best ways to influence teens' behavior? What can be done to foster and reward safe driving as normative behavior for teens? Which adolescent characteristics can work as protective factors, and how might they best be harnessed? What is known about teens' own attitudes regarding driving safety and potential solutions? What role do the media play now—how might the influence of the media and commercial vendors (such as the automotive and communications industries) be harnessed to foster responsible driving practices? What is known about the effectiveness of current media campaigns? How might law enforcement and the insurance industry play bigger, more proactive roles in improving safety?

What are the best ways to influence policy makers and the public? To the extent that the research community can reach consensus on the need for further changes in laws and public policies, as well as attitudes and expectations among parents and the public, what social marketing and other strategies have demonstrated effectiveness for this purpose in other contexts?

How are new and existing programs performing? Evaluations that encompass new findings about teenagers and driver behavior are needed to improve the quality of existing driver education programs, including advanced skills training, as well as other approaches that draw on new research on adolescent development, behavior, and decision-making processes.

What are the costs and benefits of different types of interventions? Linking specific interventions or strategies to selected costs and benefits is a daunting challenge. Large study samples are required to examine the effects of certain approaches with selected cohorts of teen populations, taking into account significant individual and demographic variables. Interventions that entail costs that accrue to individuals (such as the fees associated with driver education or the installation of new technology in automobiles) may offer major benefits to society through the reduction of injury and improvement of safety. These relationships deserve further consideration in the design of incentives and regulatory frameworks.

What policies might best address the problem of sleep deprivation? The cycles associated with teen sleep patterns are well known, but this research has not been applied in any consistent manner to the design of licensure standards, driver education programs, or public health messages for teens and their parents. Health care providers and educators are important but undeveloped assets who are in a position to guide teens and parents about the importance of adequate sleep in preventing risky and dangerous behaviors.

NEXT STEPS

This set of questions could serve as the starting point for further exploration of these complex issues. Many participants expressed the hope that additional opportunities will emerge—through new public and private partnerships—for interdisciplinary collaboration in the development of prevention strategies for teen drivers. The workshop clearly demonstrated that a wealth of information is available that has not been brought to bear on a public health issue of immense proportions.

References

Allen, J.P., Porter, M.R., McFarland, C.F., Marsh, P.A., and McElhaney, K.B. (2005). The two faces of adolescents' success with peers: Adolescent popularity, social adaptation, and deviant behavior. *Child Development, 76,* 747-760.

American Automobile Association. (2006). Teen crashes—Everyone is at risk. AAA Office of Government Relations. Available: http://www.aaaexchange.com/Assets/Files/200611814220.TeenDriversRisk2.pdf (accessed 8/25/2006).

Baker, S.P., Chen, L.H., and Guohua, L. (2006). Graduated driver licensing programs and fatal crashes of 16-year-old drivers. *Pediatrics, 118*(1), 56-62.

Cooper, D., Gillen, D., and Atkins, F. (2004). *Impacts of California's graduated licensing law of 1998.* Berkeley: University of California Institute of Transportation Studies.

D'Angelo, L.J. (2006). *Behind the wheel: A health care provider looks at teen driving.* Presentation for the Workshop on Contributions from the Behavioral and Social Sciences in Reducing and Preventing Teen Motor Crashes, May 15, National Academies, Washington, DC. Available: http://www.bocyf.org/050506.html [accessed 12/06].

Fohr, S.A., Layde, P.M., and Guse, C.E. (2005). Graduated driver licensing in Wisconsin: Does it create safer drivers? *Wisconsin Medical Journal, 104,* 31-36.

Glad, A. (1988). *Phase II driver education, effect on accident risk.* Oslo: Norway Transport Institute.

Gregersen, N.P. (1996). *Young car drivers: Why are they over represented in car accidents? How can driver training improve their situation?* (VTI Rapport 409A). Linkoping: Swedish National Road and Transport Institute.

Insurance Institute for Highway Safety. (2006). *Fatality facts 2005: Teenagers.* Highway Loss Data Institute. Available: http://www.iihs.org/research/fatality_facts/teenagers.html (accessed 7/21/2006).

Insurance Institute for Highway Safety. (2004). *Fatality facts 2004: Older people.* Available at http://www.iihs.org/research/fatality_facts/olderpeople.html (accessed 4/24/2006).

Jones, B. (1993). *The effectiveness of skid-car training for teenage novice drivers in Oregon.* Salem: Oregon Drive and Motor Vehicle Services.

Lerner, R.M., and Steinberg, L. (2004). *Handbook of adolescent psychology* (2nd edition). Hoboken, NJ: John Wiley and Sons.

Luciana, M., Conklin, H.M., Hooper, C.J., and Yarger, R.S. (2005). The development of nonverbal working memory and executive control processes in adolescents. *Child Development, 76*,(3), 697-712.

Masten, S.V., and Hagge, R.A. (2004). Evaluation of California's graduated driver licensing program. *Journal of Safety Research, 35*, 523-535.

Mayhew, D., and Simpson, H. (1997). *Effectiveness and role of driver education and training in a graduated licensing system.* Ottawa, Ontario: Traffic Injury Research Foundation.

Mayhew, D.R., Simpson, H.M., and Pak, A. (2003). Changes in collision rates among novice drivers during the first months of driving. *Accident Analysis and Prevention, 35*, 683-691.

McCartt, A.T., Shabanova, V.I., and Leaf, W.A. (2003). Driving experience, crashes and traffic citations of teenage beginning drivers. *Accident Analysis and Prevention, 35*(3), 311-320.

McKnight, J.A., and McKnight, S.A. (2003). Young novice drivers: Careless or clueless. *Accident Analysis and Prevention, 35*, 921-925.

Mokdad, A.H., Marks, J.S., Stroup, D.F., and Gerberding, J.L. (2004). Actual causes of death in the United States, 2000. *Journal of the American Medical Association, 291*(10), 1238-1245.

National Center for Health Statistics. (2003). *Top 10 leading causes of death in the United States for 2003, by age group.* Centers for Disease Control and Prevention. Available: http://www-nrd.nhtsa.dot.gov/pdf/nrd-30/NCSA/RNotes/2006/810568.pdf (accessed 7/21/2006).

National Center for Injury Prevention and Control. (2006). *Teen drivers: Fact sheet.* Centers for Disease Control and Prevention. Available: http://www.cdc.gov/ncipc/factsheets/teenmvh.htm (accessed 7/13/2006).

National Highway Traffic Safety Administration. (2006a). *Traffic safety facts 2004: A compilation of motor vehicle crash data from the fatality analysis reporting system and the general estimates system.* Available: http://www-nrd.nhtsa.dot.gov/pdf/nrd-30/NCSA/TSFAnn/TSF2004.pdf (accessed 10/02/2006).

National Highway Traffic Safety Administration. (2006b). *Traffic safety facts 2003 data: Young drivers.* DOT HS 810 568. Available: http://www-nrd.nhtsa.dot.gov/pdf/nrd-30/NCSA/TSF2003/809774.pdf (accessed 8/24/2006).

National Highway Traffic Safety Administration. (2006c). *Traffic safety facts 2004 data: Young drivers.* DOT HS 809 918. Available: http://www-nrd.nhtsa.dot.gov/pdf/nrd-30/NCSA/TSF2004/809918.pdf (accessed 8/24/2006).

National Research Council and Institute of Medicine. (2004). *Reducing underage drinking: A collective responsibility.* Committee on Developing a Strategy to Reduce and Prevent Underage Drinking. Board on Children, Youth, and Families, Division of Behavioral and Social Sciences and Education. R.J. Bonnie and M.E. O'Connell, Eds. Washington, DC: The National Academies Press.

National Research Council and Institute of Medicine. (2006). *A study of interactions: Emerging issues in the science of adolescence, Workshop summary.* A. Beatty and R. Chalk,

Rapporteurs. Program Committee for a Workshop on the Synthesis of Research on Adolescent Health and Development. Board on Children, Youth, and Families, Division of Behavioral and Social Sciences and Education. Washington, DC: The National Academies Press.

National Sleep Foundation. (2006). *2006 Sleep in America poll: Summary findings*. Washington, DC: National Sleep Foundation. Available: http://www.sleepfoundation. org/_content/hottopics/2006_summary_of_findings.pdf (accessed 9/1/2006).

Ohio Department of Public Safety. (2001). An evaluation of Ohio's graduated driver license law. Columbus: Office of the Governor's Highway Safety Representative, Ohio Department of Public Safety.

Pack, A.I., Pack, A.M., Rodgman, E., et al. (1995). Characteristics of crashes attributed to the driver having fallen asleep. *Accident Analysis and Prevention, 27*(6), 769-775.

Preusser, D.F. (1995). Licensing practices and crash risk in the United States. In H.M. Simpson (ed.), *New to the road: Reducing the risks for young motorists* (pp. 87-94). Proceedings of the First Annual International Symposium of the Youth Enhancement Service, UCLA, June 8-11, Los Angeles.

Preusser, D.F. (2002). BAC and fatal crash risk. In *Proceedings of the 16th International Conference on Alcohol, Drugs and Traffic Safety*. Montreal, Canada, August 4-9.

Preusser, D.F. (2006). *Young driver crash risk*. Presentation for the Workshop on Contributions from the Behavioral and Social Sciences in Reducing and Preventing Teen Motor Crashes, May 15, National Academies, Washington, DC. Available: http://www.bocyf. org/050506.html [accessed 12/06].

Preusser, D.F., Ferguson, S.A., and Williams, A.F. (1998). The effect of teenage passengers on the fatal crash risk of teenage drivers. *Accident Analysis and Prevention, 30*(2), 217-222.

Rice, T.M., Peek-Asa, C., and Kraus, J.F. (2004). Effects of California graduated driver licensing program. *Journal of Safety Research, 35*, 375-381.

Romer, D. (ed.). (2003). *Reducing adolescent risk: Toward an integrated approach*. Thousand Oaks, CA: Sage.

Shope, J.T., and Molnar, L.J. (2004). Michigan's graduated driver licensing program: Evaluation of the first four years. *Journal of Safety Research, 35*, 337-344.

Stock, J.R., Weaver, J.K., Ray, H.W., Brink, J.R., and Sadoff, M.G. (1983). *Evaluation of safe performance secondary school driver education curriculum demonstration project*. (Final Report, DOT HS 806 568, National Highway Traffic Safety Administration.) Washington, DC: U.S. Department of Transportation.

Transport Research Centre. (2006). *Young drivers: The road to safety*. Paris: Organisation for Economic Co-operation and Development.

Transportation Research Board. (1989). *Special report 224: Safety belts, airbags, and child restraints*. Washington, DC: Transportation Research Board, National Research Council.

Transportation Research Board. (2003). *Special report 278: Buckling up: Technologies to increase seat belt use*. Washington, DC: Transportation Research Board, National Research Council.

Treat, J.R., Tumbas, N.S., McDonald, S.T., Shinar, D., Hume, R.D., Mayer, R.E., et al. (1979). *Tri-level study of the causes of traffic accidents: Final report vol. I. Causal factor tabulation and assessments* (DOT-805 085). Bloomington: Indiana University, Institute for Research in Public Safety.

Ulmer, R.G., Preusser, D.F., Williams, A.F., Ferguson, S.A., and Farmer, C.M. (2000). Effect of Florida's graduated licensing program on the crash rate of teenage drivers. *Accident Analysis and Prevention, 32,* 527-532.

Williams, A.F. (2006). Young driver risk factors: Successful and unsuccessful approaches for dealing with them and an agenda for the future. *Injury Prevention, 12*(Suppl 1), 14-18.

Williams, A.F., Weinberg, K., Fields, M., and Ferguson, S.A. (1995). *Current requirements for getting a driver's license in the United States.* Arlington, VA: Insurance Institute for Highway Safety.

Winston, E.K. (2006). *Response to workshop panel 1.* Presentation for the Workshop on Contributions from the Behavioral and Social Sciences in Reducing and Preventing Teen Motor Crashes, May 15, National Academies, Washington, DC. Available: http://www.bocyf.org/050506.html [accessed 12/06].

Winston, F.K., and Senserrick, T.M. (2006). Competent independent driving as an archetypal task of adolescence. *Injury Prevention, 12*(Suppl 1), 11-13.

Young, K. (1993). *Workshop to identify training requirements designed to reduce young driver risk taking and improve decision making skills.* (National Highway Traffic Safety Administration.)Washington, DC: U.S. Department of Transportation.

Appendix

Workshop Agenda and Participants

**Contributions from the Behavioral and Social Sciences in
Reducing and Preventing Teen Motor Crashes**

**Workshop
May 15-16, 2006**

**Board on Children, Youth, and Families
and the
Transportation Research Board**

**The National Academies
Washington, DC**

**Meeting Goals: Provide an update and engage in discussion on the
following questions:**

(1)   How do theories and evidence from the behavioral, cognitive,
social, health, and biological sciences inform understanding of the risk factors that increase teen motor vehicle crashes and the protective factors that
reduce such crashes?

(2)   How can theories and evidence from the behavioral, cognitive,
social, health, and biological sciences inform improved prevention, program, and policy interventions to reduce risky teen motor vehicle driving
behaviors, as well as promote responsible teen driving?

(3)   What research and interventions are most likely to advance teen
motor vehicle safety over the short and long term?

Monday, May 15, 2006

Welcome, Introductions, and Overview of the Workshop
- What is the task of the committee?
- Workshop format
- What do we hope to learn from this workshop?

*Robert Graham, M.D., University of Cincinnati College of Medicine/
Workshop Moderator, Committee Chair*

Panel 1: Teens Behind the Wheel
- Description of the problem (crashes, injuries, magnitude, forecast).
- Complexity of driving and crash avoidance, particularly for novice drivers.
- How is driving different for teens (e.g., age, inexperience, crash factors)?
- What do we know about contributing factors to teen driver crashes (e.g., age, gender, experience, time of day, passengers, alcohol, seat belts)?
- What is the set of cognitive and motor skills that must be learned in order to be a safe driver?

*David Preusser, Ph.D., Preusser Research Group
A. James McKnight, Ph.D., Transportation Research Associates*

Respondent:
*Flaura Winston, M.D., Ph.D., Children's Hospital of Philadelphia/
Committee Member*

Discussion and Q & A

Panel 2: Adolescent Development

(A) Physical Characteristics of Adolescents
- How does the adolescent brain and its development affect teen driving?
- How do adolescent sleep patterns and sleep needs affect teen driving?

Abigail Baird, Ph.D., Dartmouth College, School of Psychological and Brain Sciences
Mary Carskadon, Ph.D., Brown University

Discussion and Q & A

(B) Adolescent Relationships
- What are the characteristics of adolescent peer relationships and the influence of these relationships on adolescent decision making and risk-taking?
- What are the characteristics of adolescent relationships with parents and the influence of these relationships on adolescent decision making and risky behavior?
- How do adolescents perceive adult authority and what is the influence of these relationships on adolescent decision making and risky behavior?
- How do these adolescent social relationships influence risky behavior?

Sara Kinsman, M.D., M.S.C.E., Children's Hospital of Philadelphia
Joseph Allen, Ph.D., University of Virginia
Bruce Simons-Morton, Ed.D., NICHD/NIH

Discussion and Q & A

(C) Adolescent Behavior: Risky Behavior and Decision Making
- What do we know about social and behavioral research on adolescent risky behavior, sensation-seeking, and reckless behavior?
- What research guides our understanding of self-regulated and executive functioning during adolescence?
- What factors and settings influence how adolescents make decisions?
- How do patterns of adolescent risky behavior and decision making influence teen driving and teen driving interventions?

Ronald Dahl, M.D., Staunton Professor of Psychiatry and Pediatrics, University of Pittsburgh
Julie Downs, Ph.D., Carnegie Mellon University, Department of Social and Decision Sciences

Respondent:
Donald Fisher, Ph.D., University of Massachusetts/Committee Member

Adolescent Development: Cross-Cutting Discussion

William DeJong, Ph.D., Boston University/Committee Member

Panel 3: Current Approaches to the Teen Driving Problem

- Education: What approaches to improve teen driving outcomes have been tried in the U.S. and internationally (e.g., guidance for parents, driver education)?
- Laws and enforcement: What approaches to improve teen driving outcomes have been tried in the U.S. and internationally (e.g., seat belt regulations, alcohol policies, license suspension/revocation policies)?
- Public health/social policy: What approaches to improve teen driving outcomes have been tried in the U.S. and internationally (graduated licensing, mandated hours of driving practice, health care provider interventions, health education)?
- What has worked, what has not, and what has not been evaluated?
- What has been the impact of these policies?

Anne McCartt, Ph.D., Insurance Institute for Highway Safety
Robert Foss, Ph.D., University of North Carolina
Richard Compton, Ph.D., Director, NHTSA
Lawrence D'Angelo, M.D., M.P.H., F.S.A.M., Children's Hospital, Washington, DC

Respondents:
Ruth Shults, Ph.D., Centers for Disease Control and Prevention
Allan F. Williams, Ph.D., Bethesda, M.D./Committee Member

Discussion and Q & A

Panel 4: Emerging Driving Technology
- What technologies exist to enhance training and feedback?
- What is the field experience of driver technology and its influence on teens and driving?

Max Donath, Ph.D., Intelligent Transportation Systems Institute, University of Minnesota
R. Wade Allen, MS, Systems Technology, Inc.
John Lee, Ph.D., University of Iowa/Committee Member

Discussion and Q & A

Adjourn

Tuesday, May 16, 2006

Welcome and Overview of Day 2

Robert Graham, M.D., Moderator, Committee Chair

Panel 5: Teen Driving Current Challenges
- To what extent are current policies and interventions informed by issues of adolescent development? How might they be revised to take into account teen driving and adolescent development?
- What role can parents, teachers, and other adults play in building driving competencies and reducing risky behaviors among teens?
- What role can the media and public messaging about driving play in building driving competencies and reducing risky behaviors among teens?
- What areas of teen driving risk have we missed in the presentations and discussion?
- What research is needed to move the field forward?

Richard Catalano, Ph.D., University of Washington, Social Development Research Group
Sue Ferguson, Ph.D., Insurance Institute for Highway Safety

Respondent:
Jean Shope, Ph.D., University of Michigan/Committee Member

Discussion and Q & A

Discussant Reports and Group Discussion

James Hedlund, Ph.D., President, Highway Safety North
Daniel Keating, Ph.D., University of Michigan/Committee Member

Wrap-up

Robert Graham, M.D.

Adjourn

WORKSHOP PARTICIPANTS

Joseph P. Allen, Ph.D., Department of Psychology, University of Virginia

R. Wade Allen, M.S., Systems Technology, Inc., Hawthorne, CA

Jon Antin, VA Tech Transportation Institute, Blacksburg

Randy Atkins, National Academy of Engineering, Washington, DC

Abigail Baird, Ph.D., Department of Psychological and Brain Sciences, Dartmouth College

Brian K. Barber, Ph.D., Department of Child and Family Studies, University of Tennessee

Thomas Bevan, dNovus RDI, Atlanta, GA

Stephanie Binder, National Highway Traffic Safety Administration, Washington, DC

C. Raymond Bingham, University of Michigan Transportation Research Institute, Ann Arbor, MI

Scott Brawley, National Sleep Foundation, Washington, DC

Claire D. Brindis, Dr.P.H., National Adolescent Health Information Center, University of California, San Francisco

John Brock, Anteon, Washington, DC

Alan Brown, Joshua Brown Foundation, Kennesaw, GA

B. Bradford Brown, Ph.D., Department of Educational Psychology, University of Wisconsin

Melissa Burns, Veritas, Washington, DC

Alex Cardinali, Nissan North America, Inc., Herndon, VA

Mary Carskadon, Ph.D., Department of Psychiatry and Human Behavior, Brown Medical School

Richard F. Catalano, Ph.D., Social Development Research Group, School of Social Work, University of Washington

Rosemary Chalk, Board on Children, Youth, and Families, National Research Council and Institute of Medicine, Washington, DC

Lori Cohen, American Association of Motor Vehicle Administrators, Arlington, VA

Bill Combs, Teen Driver Safety, Bethesda, MD

Richard Compton, Ph.D., Traffic Injury Control, National Highway Traffic Safety Administration, Washington, DC

Brian Cox, University of Virginia, Charlottesville, VA

Daniel Cox, UVA Health Systems Center, Charlottesville, VA

Ronald E. Dahl, M.D., Child and Adolescent Sleep/Neurobehavioral Laboratory, Western Psychiatric Institute and Clinic and the University of Pittsburgh

Vicki Dang, Student, George Washington University, Washington, DC

Lawrence J. D'Angelo, M.D., M.P.H., Center for Community Pediatric Health, Children's National Medical Center, Washington, DC

Maggie Davis, UVA Health Systems Center, Charlottesville, VA

William DeJong, Ph.D., School of Public Health, Boston University

Thomas Dingus, Virginia Tech Transportation Institute, Blacksburg, VA

T. Bella Dinh-Zarr, American Automobile Association National Office, Washington, DC

Max Donath, Ph.D., Intelligent Transportation Systems Institute, University of Minnesota

Nancy Donovan, Government Accountability Office, Washington, DC

Julie S. Downs, Ph.D., Department of Social and Decision Sciences, Carnegie Mellon University

Darrel Drobnich, National Sleep Foundation, Washington, DC

Susan Duchak, Allstate Foundation, Northbrook, IL

Patricia Ellison-Potter, National Highway Traffic Safety Administration, Washington, DC

Kathleen Ethier, Centers for Disease Control and Prevention, Atlanta, GA

Sue Ferguson, Ph.D., Insurance Institute for Highway Safety, Arlington, VA

Mighty Fine, American Public Health Association, Washington, DC

Donald L. Fisher, Ph.D., Human Performance Laboratory, Department of Mechanical and Industrial Engineering, University of Massachusetts, Amherst

Scott Fisher, National Association of County and City Health Officials, Washington, DC

Robert D. Foss, Ph.D., Center for the Study of Young Drivers, Highway Safety Research Center, University of North Carolina

Mark Freedman, Westat, Rockville, MD

John Frooshani, Nissan North America, Inc., Herndon, VA

John Gardenier, Centers for Disease Control and Prevention, Vienna, VA

Turkan Gardenier, Pragmatica Corporation, Vienna, VA

Jay Giedd, National Institute of Mental Health, Bethesda, MD

Anne Ginn, General Motors, Warren, MI

Charity Goodman, Government Accountability Office, Washington, DC

Jennifer Appleton Gootman, Board on Children, Youth, and Families, National Research Council and Institute of Medicine, Washington, DC

Robert Graham, M.D., Department of Family Medicine, College of Medicine, University of Cincinnati

Allen Greenberg, U.S. Department of Transportation, Washington, DC

Jeff Greenberg, Ford Motor Company, Dearborn, MI

Lauren Hafner, Children's Hospital of Philadelphia

Bonnie L. Halpern-Felsher, Ph.D., Division of Adolescent Medicine, University of California, San Francisco

Christian Hanna, Children's Safety Center, Marshfield, WI

James Hedlund, Ph.D., Highway Safety North, Ithaca, NY

Russell Henk, Texas Transportation Institute, San Antonio, TX

Marci Hertz, Centers for Disease Control and Prevention, Atlanta, GA

William Horrey, Liberty Mutual Research Institute for Safety, Hopkinton, MA

James Jenness, Westat, Rockville, MD

Christene Jennings, Automotive Coalition for Traffic Safety, Inc., Arlington, VA

Ewa Kalicka, Children's Hospital of Philadelphia

Daniel P. Keating, Ph.D., Center for Human Growth and Development, University of Michigan

Shimrit Keddem, Children's Hospital of Philadelphia

Wendy Keenan, Board on Children, Youth, and Families, National Research Council and Institute of Medicine, Washington, DC

Tara Kelley-Baker, PIRE, Calverton, MD

Sara Kinsman, M.D., M.S.C.E., Division of Adolescent Medicine, Children's Hospital of Philadelphia

Peter Kissinger, AAA Foundation for Traffic Safety, Washington, DC

Sheila Klauer, VA Tech Transportation Institute, Blacksburg, VA

Terry Kline, Eastern Kentucky University, Richmond, KY

John D. Lee, Ph.D., Department of Mechanical and Industrial Engineering, University of Iowa

Suzie Lee, VA Tech Transportation Institute, Blacksburg, VA

Neil Lerner, Westat, Rockville, MD

Nadine Levick, Academic, New York, NY

Lawrence Lonero, Northport Associates, Cobourg, Ontario, Canada

John Lundell, Injury Prevention Research Center, University of Iowa, Iowa City

Neal Martin, South Carolina Department of Health and Environmental Control, Columbia, SC

Daniel R. Mayhew, M.A., Traffic Injury Research Foundation, Ottawa, Ontario, Canada

Anne T. McCartt, Ph.D., Insurance Institute for Highway Safety, Arlington, VA

Daniel V. McGehee, University of Iowa, Iowa City

Mary Pat McKay, George Washington University, Washington, DC

A. James McKnight, Ph.D., Transportation Research Associates, Annapolis, MD

Justin McNaull, American Automobile Association, Washington, DC

Jacqueline Milani, Center for Injury Research and Policy, Johns Hopkins University, Baltimore, MD

Peter Moe, Maryland Highway Safety Office, Hanover, MD

Frederik Mottola, National Institute for Driver Behavior, Cheshire, CT

Cheryl Neverman, National Highway Traffic Safety Administration, Washington, DC

Erik Olsen, National Institute of Child Health and Human Development, Bethesda, MD

Marie Claude Ouimet, National Institute of Child Health and Human Development, Bethesda, MD

Richard Pain, Transportation Research Board, Washington, DC

Mike Perel, National Highway Traffic Safety Administration, Washington, DC

Kathleen Perkins, West Virginia University, Morgantown, WV

Val Pezoldt, Texas Transportation Institute, San Antonio, TX

Alexander Pollatsek, University of Massachusetts, Amherst, MA

David Preusser, Ph.D., Preusser Research Group, Inc., Trumbull, CT

Deborah Quackenbush, Raydon Corporation, Daytona Beach, FL

Alex Quistberg, Children's Hospital of Philadelphia

Katherine Redding, U.S. Department of Health and Human Services, Washington, DC

Barbara Rogers, Centers for Disease Control and Prevention, Washington, DC

Carol W. Runyan, Ph.D., Injury Prevention Research Center, University of North Carolina

Meredith St. Louis, South Carolina Department of Health and Environmental Control, Columbia, SC

Teresa Senserrick, Children's Hospital of Philadelphia

Karen Sherwood, Partnership for Prevention, Washington, DC

Jean Thatcher Shope, Ph.D., Transportation Research Institute, University of Michigan

Ruth Shults, Ph.D., M.P.H., Center for Injury Prevention and Control, Centers for Disease Control and Prevention, Atlanta, GA

Amy Sievers, Iowa Department of Transportation, Des Moines, IA

Bruce Simons-Morton, Ed.D., M.P.H., Prevention Research Branch, National Institute of Child Health and Human Development, Bethesda, MD

Renee Slick, Kansas State University, Manhattan, KS

Susan Solomon, Office of Behavioral and Social Science Research, National Institutes of Health, Bethesda, MD

Loren Staplin, TransAnalytics, LLC, Kulpsville, PA

Kevin Techau, Iowa Dept of Public Safety, Des Moines, IA

Anne Titler, Pennsylvania Department of Transportation, Harrisburg, PA

Deborah Trombley, National Safety Council, Itasca, IL

Matthew Trowbridge, University of Michigan, Ann Arbor, MI

Steve Tudor, Iowa Department of Transportation, Des Moines, IA

Robert Voas, PIRE, Calverton, MD

Penny Wells, Students Against Drunk Driving, Inc., Marlborough, MA

Joel Whitaker, Beverage Daily News, Burtonsville, MD

John White, American Automobile Association, Heathrow, FL

Brad Wible, Office of Behavioral and Social Science Research, National Institutes of Health, Bethesda, MD

Pat Wilder, Joshua Brown Foundation, Kennesaw, GA

Allan F. Williams, Ph.D., Consultant, Bethesda, MD

Flaura Koplin Winston, M.D., Ph.D., Center for Injury Research and Prevetion, Children's Hospital of Philadelphia

Dianne Wolman, Institute of Medicine, Washington, DC